COVID-19, the Great Recession and Young Adult Identity Development

This book offers a paradigm shift in the framing of identity development by advancing a new, shock-sensitive framework for diverse young adult identity development after high school.

The author builds on the critical theoretical contributions of Urie Bronfenbrenner and Margaret Beale Spencer that highlight the person-context nature of development and the dynamic nature of vulnerability, risk, and coping. The inclusive, policy-relevant theoretical approach emerges from the author's mixed-methods study that examines the context-dependent identity development experiences of young adults. The book also accounts for the unique person-context dynamics during the Great Recession and COVID-19 global shocks that drive how diverse young adults make meaning of risk as they cope with the shock-related disruptions on their individual postsecondary journeys toward building their adult identities. Given that the qualitative interview component of the study occurred during the COVID-19 pandemic, this research offers a unique, in-real-time vantage point from participants who are making meaning of their choices and decisions as the shock was underway. The book also tracks the heightened importance of online tools during this period and the implications of virtual contexts where developmental activities are pursued, such as online education, work, and socializing.

Advancing a new, shock-sensitive, interdisciplinary theory of identity development in postsecondary journeys of diverse young adults, it will appeal to scholars and students at the graduate level working across psychology, human development, educational psychology, sociology of education, and public policy.

Bronwyn Nichols Lodato is an Assistant Professor in the Department of Education and the Department of African and African-American Studies at Washington University in St. Louis, USA.

Explorations in Developmental Psychology Series

Developmental Neuropsychology
Janna Glozman

Indigenous Adolescent Development
Psychological, Social and Historical Contexts
Les B. Whitbeck, Kelley J. Sittner Hartshorn and Melissa L. Walls

Learning from Picturebooks
Research from Cognitive Psychology, Early Literacy, and Child Developmental Studies
Edited by Bettina Kummerling-Meibauer, Jörg Meibauer, Kerstin Nachtigäller and Katharina Rohlfing

Development from Adolescence to Early Adulthood
A Dynamic Systemic Approach to Transitions and Transformations
Marion Kloep, Leo B. Hendry, Rachel Taylor and Ian Stuart-Hamilton

Teachers, Learners, Modes of Practice
Theory and Methodology for Identifying Knowledge Development
David Kirk Dirlam

Children's Books, Brain Development, and Language Acquisition
Ralf Thiede

Child Development Mediated by Trauma
The Dark Side of International Adoption
Boris Gindis

Researching Child-Dog Relationships and Narratives in the Classroom
Rhythms of Posthuman Childhoods
Donna Carlyle

COVID-19, the Great Recession and Young Adult Identity Development
Shock-Sensitive Dynamic Ecological Systems Theory
Bronwyn Nichols Lodato

COVID-19, the Great Recession and Young Adult Identity Development

Shock-Sensitive Dynamic Ecological Systems Theory

Bronwyn Nichols Lodato

Routledge
Taylor & Francis Group
NEW YORK AND LONDON

First published 2024
by Routledge
605 Third Avenue, New York, NY 10158

and by Routledge
4 Park Square, Milton Park, Abingdon, Oxon, OX14 4RN

Routledge is an imprint of the Taylor & Francis Group, an informa business

ISBN: 978-1-032-51345-4 (hbk)
ISBN: 978-1-032-73025-7 (pbk)
ISBN: 978-1-003-40484-2 (ebk)

DOI: 10.4324/9781003404842

Typeset in Times New Roman
by Apex CoVantage, LLC

Contents

Acknowledgments

I am eternally grateful to my family for supporting me from the conceptualization of this research study through the completion of this book. Prof. Raymond Lodato, my rock, and Gabriel, Matthew, and Nicholas, you are a constant source of inspiration; Dr. Andrea Nichols, Earl Nichols, Suzanne Nichols, and Jonathan Nichols and children, thank you for your enduring patience, love, and wellspring of needed support and laughter during moments of struggle; and the boundless encouragement from Dr. Frank Lodato, Patricia Lodato, Dr. Denise Lodato, and Janice Lodato and family was a critical source of support for which I am deeply appreciative.

I am also immensely appreciative of the intellectual support and mentorship from my advisors and many supportive scholars who provided the right words of encouragement at the right time as I navigated this research study and book project. These persons span the social sciences and varied theoretical and disciplinary traditions whose feedback and insights enriched my intellectual development beyond measure. I am especially appreciative of the enduring support of this research from Prof. Margaret Beale Spencer, Prof. Walter Allen, Prof. Lindsey Richland, Prof. Richard Taub, and Prof. Eman Abdelhabi and the administrative skills of Mr. Oliver Garland. Thank you to intellectual touchstones and supporters over the years, including Prof. Bill Trent, Prof. Ed St. John, Prof. Ralph Lerner, Dr. Jack Buckley, Prof. Will Shadish and Prof. Leon Forrest. A special thank you to Ms. Karen and Dr. Allan Rechtschaffen for their support and Dr. Katherine and Mr. James Mann for their generosity of space and time. The technical support of staff at the University of Chicago's Regenstein Library provided tremendous guidance and expertise that was invaluable, and I extend a special thanks to Ms. Colleen Mullarkey for crucial guidance at critical points.

The primary research for this book was aided by the support of grants from the American Psychological Association's Commission on Ethnic Minority Recruitment, Retention, and Training in Psychology program; the University of Chicago's Division of the Social Sciences Doctoral Research Innovation Fund; and the Bernice Neugarten Scholarship Endowment Award from the Department of Comparative Human Development at the University of Chicago. The ideas and conclusions presented here in this book are solely those of the author.

The conduct of theoretically motivated social science research studies necessitates involvement from multiple actors who help advance the research from initial participant recruitment to data analysis steps. I am appreciative of the helpful staff at the Institute for Social Research at the University of Michigan in providing guidance on accessing and utilizing the Panel Survey of Income Dynamics Transition to Adulthood dataset. I commend their foresight in capturing crucial insights on the Great Recession as it was underway, and I look forward to further analyses of these rich data in my future research endeavors. For the qualitative component, I was the recipient of the tremendous kindness of individuals and organizations from across the country who worked directly with me to conduct outreach and recruitment efforts for participants. I thank them for their crucial support of the study during a period of immense difficulty as the COVID-19 global pandemic was raging across the globe. Once the data were collected, the immense task of combing through the interviews required supportive assistants. The research assistants who aided in the coding process, with all the recursive steps involved, were crucial in helping organize the data to better facilitate identification of key findings that addressed the study's motivating research questions.

This book would not be possible without the commitment, candor, and brilliance of the young adults who generously gave of their time to participate in this study during a period of great tumult in their lives. I am appreciative of the time they gave to me to share important details about who they were as individuals, their journeys, and how they were coping through the pandemic shock. I have worked diligently to bring their voices to the fore in this book in hopes of enlightening us all on the unique attributes of shocks on developmental trajectories.

Thank you to Routledge and its amazing editorial staff. They were very patient with me as I prepared this book and provided great support as I navigated the twists and turns of publication. (I am particularly grateful to Alice Salt and Stuti Das for their gracious and brilliant support.)

It is my hope that the diverse young adult voices and the insights presented in this book permit new approaches to enhance and support young adult identity development in dynamic contexts.

Bronwyn Nichols Lodato, PhD
Summer, 2023

1 What Happens When the World Stops?

Within a 20-year period, the world experienced asymmetric events, or shocks, that disrupted the social fabric and economic systems in societies around the globe. The Great Recession (2007–2009) and the COVID-19 pandemic (2020–2023), which sparked a linked economic recession, were global in nature with enduring effects experienced at the individual, human level. In the United States (U.S.), the implications of these shocks on individuals re-framed how to understand human developmental pathways underway during and between these shock events. Indeed, the economic and health impacts disrupted governing assumptions about the effectiveness of societal systems to respond to and serve human needs. This, then, opens the question of how systemic shocks alter understanding of how individuals navigate risks and secure supports, which serve as protective factors that aid in navigating their lives in varied social contexts over time. This shift in the underlying assumptions about proper functions of institutions, organizations and processes that undergird the social environments where developmental psychological tasks occur, i.e., the psychosocial environments, merit interrogation. Specifically, it is important to understand the impact of the Great Recession and COVID-19 shock events on the stability of human developmental contexts. Relatedly, this consideration of broad destabilization, then, invites scrutiny of the implications for young adults undertaking the work of identity development (e.g., meeting new obligations aligned with advancing maturity; engaging in tasks in pursuit of their educational and career goals) when a shock disrupts their living learning, and working environments.

When examining the Great Recession and COVID-19 pandemic, then it is important to assess how these events wrought havoc on individuals' pathways, disrupting the person-context dynamics that advance developmental activities already underway. The pandemic posed a particularly acute threat to human health and safety, as the quickly spreading virus caused the worst public health emergency experienced in over a century. During the Great Recession, the economic toll was second only to the Great Depression for the impact on jobs, housing and beyond. The U.S. housing market graphically illustrates the deep harm wrought by the Great Recession, with the toll experienced literally

DOI: 10.4324/9781003404842-1

on the home front for millions of people. The value of homes, a key indicator of and a path to generation of economic and social stability in the U.S., dropped at a rate not seen since after World War II translating into an estimated loss of $7 trillion in home equity, the amount of wealth generated in home ownership that belonged to the owners (Gould Ellen & Dastrup, 2012). As homeowners owed more than the value of their homes and the rate of foreclosure starts accelerated to historic highs, drops in household wealth dropped at disparate rates, with African American and Hispanic/Latino groups losing 53 percent and 66 percent of wealth, respectively, compared to White households that experienced a 16 percent reduction (*Ibid*). During the Great Recession, job losses mounted, with African Americans and Hispanic/Latino American groups being hit the hardest with the highest rates of short- and long-term unemployment (U.S. Bureau of Labor Statistics, 2012). Even after the Great Recession was declared over, many around the globe were still rebuilding from the aftermath of the economic losses and associated impacts on life trajectories years later. Home ownership rates fell, particularly for young adults (Gould Ellen & Dastrup, 2012), and lost employment income hampered building of savings foundational to long-term stability. Certainly, the rate of recovery would needed to have occurred at a pattern sensitive to the varied degrees of intensity of harm experienced in order for whole societies to return to pre-recessionary standards of living. (Please note that for many, the pre-recessionary living standards were already insufficient to meet the needs of those at or below the poverty levels.) As such, the Great Recession closed with many hardest hit further behind than at the start of the shock, having to play catch up with less. In sum, recovery was uneven: while the Great Recession was declared over in 2009, estimates track the lagging effects of the acute period of the shock occurring into 2012, with these broader implications remaining active for years to come for many who endured the shocks' worst effects (Dettling, Hsu, & Llanes, 2018).

Almost decade later, in early 2020, a virus that would become known as COVID-19 was announced as a lethal threat to humanity as a global health emergency was declared. The last pandemic that occurred at a global scale prior to COVID-19 was the Spanish Flu Epidemic of 1918, over a century earlier (Faust, Lin, & del Rio, 2020). While the world had experienced outbreaks of viruses over the years (Bird Flu, SARS, AIDS, and Ebola, the latter two among the most virulent viruses in modern times), global health monitoring and public health agencies were ill-prepared for the historic shock of COVID-19. It came seemingly out of nowhere and was highly contagious, with mere encounter with the air particulates of an infected person causing transmission of the potentially lethal virus. Furthermore, the surreptitious nature of the contagion among infected persons meant that a person could be infected and asymptomatic, inadvertently spreading the virus without knowledge, further raising mass worry that fed off a climate of high anxiety. Indeed, the mass shutdowns of schools, businesses and companies to "stop the spread" did not merely disrupt daily routines of life. The COVID-19 shutdowns transformed the very nature of existence across the globe in which moving about in lived environments to meet psychological, material, social, and existential needs was abruptly halted. An altered form of reality emerged whereby the tools and platforms on the internet became how many societies continued to function, where the flattened appearances on screens echoed the de-humanized nature of interaction. As work and education routines became digitized for many, for others who worked in industries and services deemed essential, each day was fraught with danger as these individuals carried out duties to keep basic societal functions active without adequate safety or support gear. Indeed, if global society was in a war with the COVID-19 virus, essential workers were truly the unheralded soldiers and heroes on the front lines. These persons—grocery and retail workers, medical and hospital staff, caregivers, food service workers, food supply chain employees (slaughterhouse workers, farm workers), truck drivers, train operators, and public works employees—were among those whose jobs did not move online platforms. These persons faced daily risk of infection in order to ensure basic societal functions continued. Indeed, going to work was a life and death proposition. Schools were closed, and students moved to online learning environments. For those with little to no access to the internet, digital inequity followed patterns of inequality and disinvestment already present in communities that did not have programs in place to ensure equitable access of citizens to tools to support information access and social connectivity (e.g., Chicago's map of digital inequity reveals an almost 40 percentage point difference between the highest- and lowest-resourced neighborhoods', mapping the pattern of economic and racial segregation that shapes residential patterns; University of Chicago Data Science Institute, 2022).

Science rushed to keep pace with the spread of the virus and to calm the fear it sparked in societies and communities around the globe. In the early days of the pandemic, there was no effective, population-based testing program that could ascertain the scale and nature of spread accurately, exacerbating the risk and vulnerability of human populations to exposure and sickness. Furthermore, it was a struggle to obtain good information about strategies to stay safe as misinformation spread as rapidly as the virus, with conspiracy theories abounding and even government leaders and entities singling out scientific institutions for derision to gain political advantage out of a human tragedy. The impact was heartbreakingly tragic, with families and social ties strained, severely damaged, or permanently lost from the 6,948,764 lives lost from the virus (World Health Organization, 2023). In the U.S., 1,134,300 persons died from the virus, and millions more would suffer from the debilitating long-term effects of the virus (National Center for Immunization and Respiratory Diseases [NCIRD], 2022). The particular threat to health posed by the COVID-19 pandemic cannot be overstated. Nowhere is the adverse impact of the pandemic evident than in life expectancy. Globally, life expectancy dropped by two years between 2019 and 2021, from 73 years to 71 years, ending 60 years of steady increase in life spans (The World Bank, 2023). This downward trend was agnostic to the wealth of a given country as countries regardless of wealth experienced decreases in life expectancy. In the U.S., COVID-19 accelerated downward trends in life expectancy, with overall life expectancy in the U.S. decreasing by 18 months (Arias, Tejada-Vera, Ahmad, & Kochanek, 2021), with Black and Hispanic communities experiencing the biggest drops (Andrasfay & Goldman, 2021; Rodriguez-Diaz, Guilamo-Ramos, Mena, Hall, Honermann, Crowley, Baral, Prado, Marzan-Rodriguez, Beyrer, Sullivan, & Millett, 2020; Yancy, 2020). From a research and policy perspective, longstanding theoretical and empirical assumptions rooted in an assumption of extending life spans no longer hold. The asymmetric shock of COVID-19 in particular revealed that governing theoretical and empirical approaches to evaluating psychosocial development necessitated an orientation shift: the novel health shock revealed a need to now account for a reversal of life gains for some, and a deepening of precarity already present when the shock hit for many others. This character of this dynamic reassessment is necessarily dependent upon the arrangement of privileges, power, and inequality in a given society.

Shared Vulnerability, Broad Risks, Uneven Effects

The social paradigm shifts precipitated by the Great Recession and the COVID-19 pandemic reoriented attitudes around how human needs were systemically understood and addressed, or not addressed, during periods of great risk. Social movements sparked to address social justice concerns were led primarily by young adults, highlighting economic and racial inequalities that rendered systems incapable or unprepared to cope with the human toll associated with the shocks and their aftermath. Occupy Wall Street, which emerged in response to the Great Recession, and Black Lives Matter, which gained momentum during COVID-19, were two major movements that began in the U.S. demanding that governmental and social institutions implement equitable policies that would reverse the damage wrought by systemic economic and racial inequality in order to enhance equitable and fair outcomes for all. These movements, particularly those that highlighted the overlapping, intersectional effects of normalized identity-based violence in developmental contexts (e.g., racial, ethnic, sexual orientation, gender identity), were aided by access to organizing tools, especially internet-based resources and social media, to connect geographically dispersed yet identity-linked communities in their shared concern for their futures. These became global movements to challenge power structures that exacerbated stressors and risks experienced by young adults as they embarked on journeys after high school (secondary education) to realize their goals for education, work, relationships, and beyond. The compounding effect of risks owed to crushing student debt (United States Government Accountability Office, 2022), threats to safety based on race, ethnicity, immigration status or gender identity, and the paucity of job opportunities that offered steady, livable wages translated into an unsustainable level of precarity for many, particularly young adults (see Standing, 2011). The presence of these stressors coexisting with shock conditions necessitates applying an ecological understanding of the human beings in context to facilitate a deeper investigation into identity development during psychohistoric periods disrupted by shocks. How individuals make meaning of risks informs the young adult developmental pathways pursued, with implications for identity development in particular. Furthermore, it is the presence and efficacy of available protective factors and supports that can aid in the cultivation of coping strategies in the presence of dynamic risks that emerge during shocks.

It is this collision of a shock event with individual, young adult developmental processes and trajectories that motivate this book. By understanding how young adults made meaning of the challenges and risks in their developmental contexts as they navigated their postsecondary pathways during shock periods, it is possible to advance a novel theory of development that accommodates disruptions with dynamic effects across varied social contexts. The capacity to develop adaptive coping mechanisms, then, is even more critical in order for individuals to sustain pursuit of goals that promote positive identity developmental processes among diverse young adults. The insights garnered from examining the young adulthood developmental period facilitate expansion to other life stage periods. To narrow the lens from the broad, systemic attributes of shocks as they shift contexts permits the investigation into the person-context dynamic that drive developmental trajectories. It is useful, then, to present the underlying developmental theories that facilitate this exploration.

Psychosocial Perspectives on Identity Development

Erik Erikson's Eight Stages of Psychosocial Development (Erikson, 1950, 1968) and Margaret Beale Spencer's Phenomenological Variant of Ecological Systems (PVEST; Spencer, 2006), an identity-focused cultural ecological (ICE) strength-based perspective, provide the theoretical bases for understanding human development in context over the life course. The Great Recession and COVID-19 shocks occurred as diverse young adults were progressing through the psychosocial stages of development that immediately follows adolescence. Motivated by Erikson's approach to understanding the dynamics of resolving identity crises associated with distinctive developmental stages paired with Spencer's invaluable insights on the engagement of risks and the cultivation of coping strategies in the formation of a stable positive identity by youths, this book investigates how exogenous shocks occurring in psychosocial contexts affect young adult identity development processes as they pursue postsecondary goals. This can facilitate a better understanding of how, in light of these shocks, diverse young adults make meaning of and cope with the dynamic risks and challenges they face in their postsecondary pursuits in order to support stable identity development at this life stage.

Shocks of this magnitude reveal the vulnerability of systems in which humans reside. Further, COVID-19 underscored shared human vulnerability to a potentially lethal biological pathogen. Given the life course ramifications of these shocks, it is essential to consider the context in which events occur to broaden how to understand the impact of an exogenous shock event on human development broadly and identity development specifically. Here, human development plays out across biological, social, and psychological domains in contexts that contain challenges, risks, supports, and other protective factors. PVEST advances that positive identity development is shaped by the meaning making and linked coping processes cultivated when 1) challenges and risks are encountered and 2) the degree to which protective factors can be activated to support youths meaning making. While PVEST focuses on diverse youths, it is applicable to developmental stages across the life course. As such, when considering young adults, it is important to understand that, as young adults confront risks and require supports, shocks have greater developmental significance: how does losing one's home or facing increased or exacerbated threats to health send a person into a state of high risk requiring greater resources and assets to achieve balance and support positive identity development? What are the disruptions associated with the closure of college campuses and migrating to online learning environments? What does it mean to young adults to move back home? What assets or resources are present that are capable of providing the needed supports to young adults to maneuver through particular challenges of expanded autonomy during shock periods? How exacerbated risks and challenges are engaged, either through adaptive or maladaptive coping mechanisms, can have implications for the developmental trajectories for young adults undertaking postsecondary educational pursuits.

Postsecondary Experiences

It is important to underscore the distinction between postsecondary experience and postsecondary education as engaged here: postsecondary experience refers to experiences after secondary (i.e., high school) education, which can encompass work, education, marriage, or other pathways chosen, or forced to choose, by young adults, while postsecondary education refers to an education path after high school, including degree attainment through two-year programs, four-year programs, or other postsecondary credential. Indeed Census data show that 10 percent of U.S. population hat attained an Associate's degree while 23 percent reported at 23 percent reorted a bachelor's degree as the highest credential attained (U.S. Census, 2023). Postsecondary experience and postsecondary education endeavors can be pursued in succession or simultaneously, and no individual pursuit is necessarily mutually exclusive of another. Postsecondary education and postsecondary work, then, are two pathways among many that are situated in the young adulthood phase in the life course. This distinction is a central component of the conceptual framework in which this research is situated. The attainment of postsecondary educational credential is a pathway considered critical to staging individuals for success over the life course (see Montgomery & Côte, 2003), but these shocks impacted the institutional settings where postsecondary education was pursued. As such, how young adults make meaning of their experiences and contexts, particularly how they leverage supports to cope with the myriad risks, decisions, options that were encountered as a result of the Great Recession and COVID-19 will be of consequence to life outcomes.

This introduction provides an overview of the theoretical and historical bases for this book, citing research on the effects of the Great Recession and COVID-19 as global shocks in U.S. society that introduced exacerbated risks. In order to ascertain the significance of these events in the U.S. with regard to diverse young adult development, it is necessary to apply a human development-centered theoretical approach. As such, the chapter further discusses Erikson's developmental stages across the life course and Spencer's perspective regarding the role of context in identity development with attendant risks, supports and phenomenological processes that motivate the cultivation of coping mechanisms. The introduction then reviews the noted shocks' destabilizing effects on developmental contexts. In many cases, these adverse impacts exacerbated the precarity of living conditions already destabilized by systemic inequality. The chapter closes with reflections on how the concept of human capital frames postsecondary education pursuits.

Psychosocial Development Encounters Exogenous Shocks

The period of time in which the Great Recession and COVID-19 occured overlaps with ongoing developmental crisis resolution underway among varied individuals at different stages across the life course. Erik Erikson's Theory of Psychosocial Development posits that individuals advance across Eight Stages of Development across the life course, with optimum functioning based on persons' successful resolution of the crises encountered at each stage over the life course (Erikson, 1950, 1968).

In Erikson's epigenetic model, each stage is comprised of unique experiences and engagement in activities that require the resolution of a crisis that advances a person to the next developmental stage. The developmental stages begin at infancy, advancing through early childhood (pre-toddler, toddler), adolescence (grade school, teenager), young adulthood, middle adulthood, into older adulthood. The progression through each stage is marked by a crisis or conflict that requires resolution in order for stable identity to be achieved. This is associated with confidence in and knowledge of self, connoting readiness for the next developmental stage. Each stage builds upon the previous one, with unfinished work resulting in a diffused identity when crises have not been resolved.

The advanced adolescence period is marked by role confusion, which can be summarized with the question of "who am I?". It is a period in which youths are determining for themselves what concepts of themselves they carry forward from what they learned and experienced in adolescence versus how much do they pull away from their parents, guardians, or other persons of authority to define themselves as individuals as they establish new social connections. The young adulthood stage follows adolescence, in which individuals grapple with the intimacy versus isolation conflict. For those who have completed the milestone of completing high school and entering college, the period is generally marked by anticipation of autonomy and self-discovery as the range of exploration is extended beyond the security of home or familiar environments and the institutional structure of high school. As such, the young adulthood period is marked by crises experienced by young adults in varied developmental contexts that may not be near the places where they grew up. This encourages young adults to cultivate new coping strategies to address risks encountered contributing to the achievement of stable identities for those between 18 and 20 years of age. Erikson notes the interconnectedness of these crises to ego identity development:

> The sense of ego identity, then, is the accrued confidence that the inner sameness and continuity are matched by the sameness and continuity of one's meaning for others, as evidenced in the tangible promise of a "career".
>
> (Erikson, 1968, p. 228)

The Phenomenology of Young Adulthood

Individual identity development occurs in two linked realms: first, the individual, phenomenological processes of meaning making that orients an individual's understanding of risks and supports and, second, the pathways pursued in dynamic developmental contexts to achieve personal goals and meet obligations in service to meeting one's needs and ambitions. PVEST acknowledges that identity development is anchored in the reality that as human beings, all individuals experience vulnerability. Specifically, "basic humanity makes vulnerability unavoidable; the status transcends racial, ethnic and SES [socioeconomic status] variation" (Nichols Lodato, Hall, & Spencer, 2021, p. 10).

Indeed, these phenomenological processes among diverse young adults, i.e., the meaning making of risks and access to supports to cultivate coping processes that accrue into an understanding of the self vis-à-vis coping with risks encountered in lived contexts. These contexts, in turn, are situated within time periods in which exogenous shocks occur, here termed as psychohistoric moments, impacting the identity development processes underway during the young adult developmental period. It is this interaction between phenomenological processes that contribute to identity development and contexts impacted by shocks that is of interest in this research. Effectively, what happens when a global shock coincides with the onset of crises associated with the reverberations (i.e., crises) of young adulthood milestone attainment for diverse populations? The utilization of an understanding of development as a series of psychosocial developmental stages across the life course facilitates exploration of the particularities of the person-context implications of shocks on identity development for diverse young adults. This effectively permits an understanding of the developmental implications of the unique stressors, challenges, and risks in developmental contexts that were precipitated, or exacerbated, by the Great Recession and COVID-19. There are well-founded challenges to the notion of a stage-based orientation to development where it pre-supposes a linearity to life stages and developmental tasks (Neugarten, 1973, 1976). For this research, however, the data do show a uniformity of school and work pursuits after high school that support investigating postsecondary experiences during the young adulthood phase.

At this point, it is useful to examine the significance and unique attributes of these global shocks, detailing the transformative effects they had in education and employment sectors, with a focus on the U.S. context, understood as one of many national experiences responding to and living through shocks. First, the effects of the Great Recession globally and domestically are reviewed, with an emphasis on postsecondary education and employment patterns. The review then moves to describing the implications of the COVID-19 global pandemic and documents key indicator data regarding its lethal health consequences along with insights on the simultaneous reckonings with the endemic inequality.

The Great Recession of 2008, Global Enrollment Patterns, and Young Adulthood

As noted earlier, the Great Recession was a financial shock that reverberated across the global economy with broad, deleterious effects on the housing and job markets, key indicators of economic stability in the U.S. It was precipitated by the collapse of overleveraged financial institutions that utilized unstable investment instruments that extended beyond the reach of standard fiscal oversight and regulatory frameworks. As a result, those components of markets that were heavily exposed to risk suffered catastrophic losses that resulted in bank closures, housing foreclosures, and job losses. The meltdown of the economy had a domino effect throughout the global economy, with impacts that not seen since the Great Depression (U.S. Bureau of Labor Statistics, 2012). Five years later, key statistical metrics "had yet to return to their pre-recession values" (U.S. BLS, 2012). Not surprisingly, the Great Recession accounted for profound shifts in the underlying social and economic fabric of many countries, with implications for educational and labor outcomes. A comparison among ten member countries of the Organization of Economic Cooperation and Development (OECD), including the U.S., conveys the severity of the event by presenting the increase in unemployment rates, a metric signifying country's economic health and social stability (Figure 1.1).

It is useful to interrogate assumptions about young adulthood, in a given national or cultural milieu, and the pursuit of postsecondary education during this period. Certainly, the management of simultaneous life roles for young adults, e.g., student, contributor to household, caregiver, worker, varies by country, and research shows that the sequencing of achieving milestones can vary widely. A study conducted by Billari and Liefbroer (2010) examined the transition to adulthood in Western European countries, with comparable democratic political

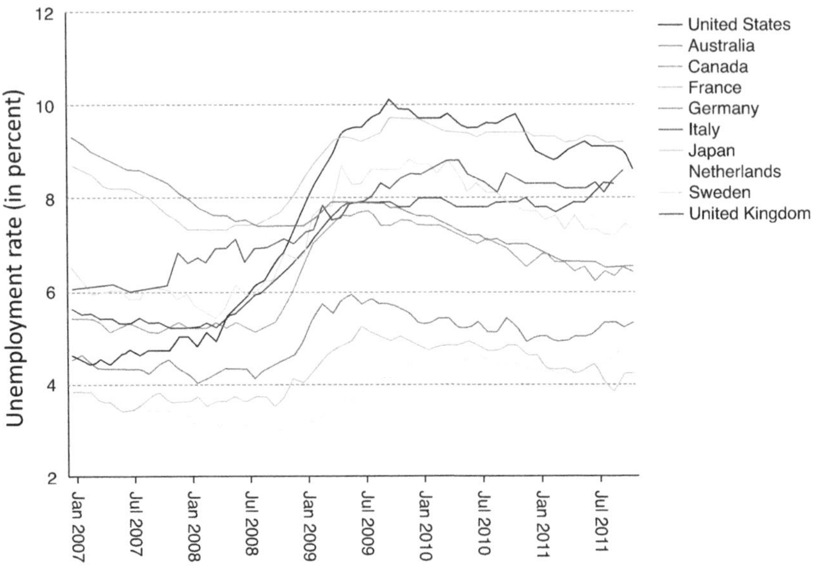

Figure 1.1 Great Recession Unemployment Rates-OECD Comparisons

Source: U.S. Bureau of Labor Statistics. (2012). The Recession of 2007–2009. Spotlight on Statistics. U.S. Department of Labor

traditions that vary but are comparable to the U.S. Their research highlighted alterations in the patterning of the achievement of milestones associated with the transition to adulthood. Additionally, Juárez and Gayet (2014) conducted a review of the literature on the role of postsecondary education in countries with developing economies, finding a misalignment of employment opportunities with the number of postsecondary education graduates who were ready to enter the labor force.

Of particular note is a consensus in research that postsecondary education can be instrumental in improving life outcomes, particularly in terms of work pursuits and wealth accumulation, with varying degrees of the "promise fulfilled" depending on the particular national context in which education is pursued (Juárez & Gayet, 2014; Montgomery & Côte, 2003; Lloyd and National Research Council, 2005). There is also research that notes how economic precarity and instability in labor markets in different countries can blunt the progression to these positive outcomes, whether countries are deemed to have developing or advanced economies (Juárez & Gayet, 2014; Chetty, Hendren, Kline, Saez, & Turner, 2014).

While in the years leading up to the Great Recession, global access to postsecondary education expanded greatly, the Great Recession laid bare the fact that a country's gross domestic product did not insulate it from the destabilizing effects of the Great Recession (Long & Adukia, 2009). Graph 1.1 depicts global trends in postsecondary (i.e., tertiary) enrollment over a 50-year period.

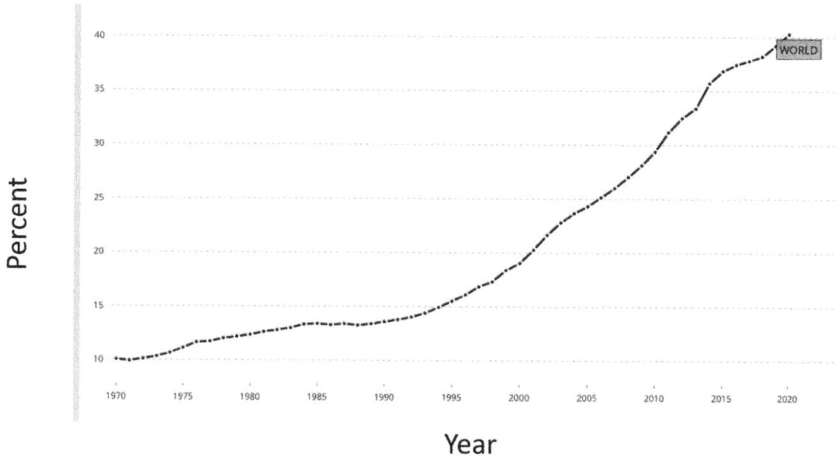

Graph 1.1 Global trends in tertiary enrollment
Source: UNESCO Institute for Statistics (UIS)

Overall, global trends in postsecondary enrollment continued upward during the years of the Great Recession. This relatively stable postsecondary enrollment pattern belies underlying shifts in the economic landscape in the U.S.

The Great Recession in the U.S. Context

To better understand its significance, it is useful to situate the Great Recession in its historical context among other recessions in the U.S. Between 1948 and 2009, the U.S. experienced ten recessions, with the 2008 recessionary event noteworthy for the depth of its impact on various sectors of society and the damage inflicted on the life trajectories of millions of people. Unemployment rates reached historic highs with the Great Recession labor market experiencing the worst downturn since the Great Depression (Elsby, Hobijn, & Sahin, 2010; Kalleberg & von Wachter, 2017) (see Figure 1.2).

The housing market bubble burst, leaving millions without stable housing (for a discussion of the recessionary housing bubble and its antecedents, see Charles, Hurst, & Notowidigdo, 2015). Effects were also felt in postsecondary education. Postsecondary institutions dealt with increased enrollment, which is consistent with the results of analyses conducted by Wright, Ramdin, and Vazquez-Colina, which showed that recessions between 1970 and 2009 did not negatively impact the overall increasing pattern of postsecondary enrollment (Wright, Ramdin, & Vazquez-Colina, 2013). This pattern of increased enrollment notwithstanding, during the Great Recession postsecondary institutions were also coping with significant drops in funding as endowments fell and states sought to cut postsecondary education appropriations in an effort to reduce overall spending (Long,

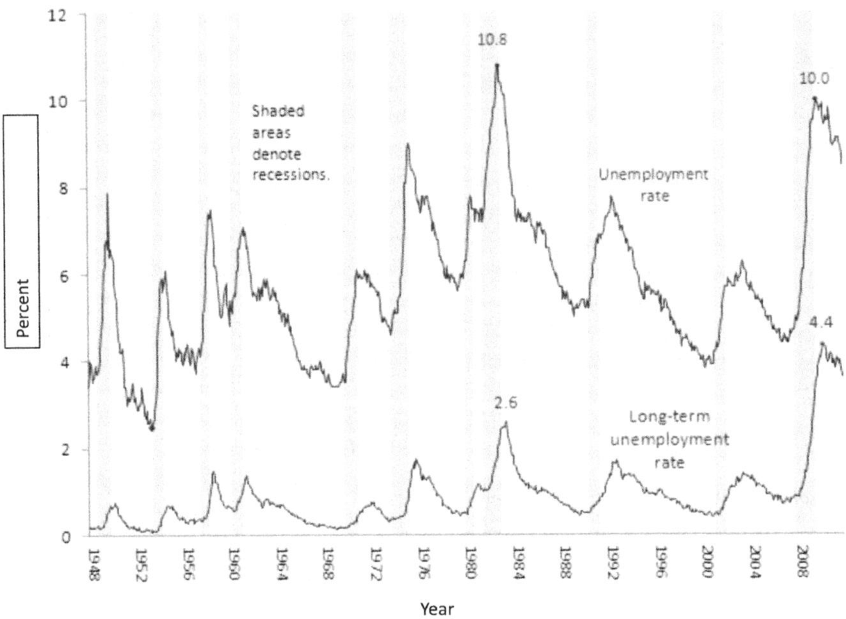

Figure 1.2 U.S. Recessionary Unemployment Rates - 1948–2008

Source: U.S. Bureau of Labor Statistics. (2012). The Recession of 2007–2009. Spotlight on Statistics. U.S. Department of Labor

2014). For sure, employment and postsecondary enrollment patterns in the U.S. endured some of the most acute effects in the fallout from the Great Recession.

Great Recession Employment and Enrollment Patterns in the U.S.

Postsecondary education is considered a crucial milestone developmentally as well as materially: research shows that attainment of a postsecondary education can lead to economic and social upward mobility in the U.S., consistent with the salutary effects noted earlier in the discussion about global enrollment patterns. According to U.S. Census data, increased earnings accompany advancing levels of educational attainment, with adults over 25 years old with less than a high school diploma earning an annual average salary of $20,361, those with a high school diploma earning $28,043, and adults with some college or a bachelor's earning $33,820 and $50,595, respectively (U.S. Census, 2015). The Great Recession, however, disrupted patterns of employment as young adults saw a decline in employment at the onset of the shock, with females employed at a lower rate than males (see Figure 1.3).

Prior to the onset of the Great Recession, there was a steady expansion of postsecondary enrollment. Between 1961 and 2007, postsecondary attainment increased substantially across both low-income and high-income groups

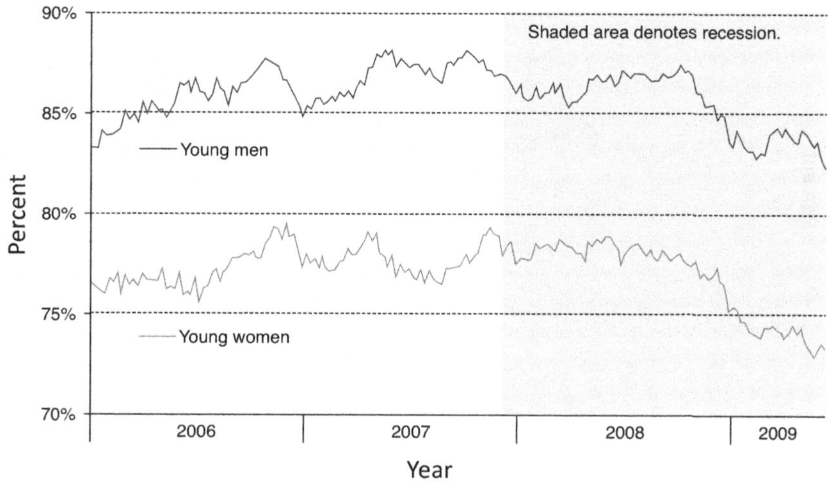

Figure 1.3 Percent of Young Adults Employed Each Week, January 2006–June 2009 (by sex)

Source: U.S. Bureau of Labor Statistics. (2012). The Recession of 2007–2009. Spotlight on Statistics. U.S. Department of Labor

Note: Categories for sex align to those utilized in the National Longitudinal Survey of Youth survey instrument.

(Bailey & Dynarski, 2011). Additionally, postsecondary education enrollment rates across different demographic groups (White, African American, Asian, Hispanic students; men and women) all rose during this pre-recessionary period (*Ibid.*). Even in the face of the economic shock, research has found that the Great Recession may have had positive effects on college enrollment and completion (Long, 2014). Bridget Terry Long found that rather than causing a disruption in the pursuit of postsecondary education, college enrollment, particularly for underrepresented students from racially and ethnically diverse backgrounds, actually increased during the Great Recession. Figure 1.4 presents the upward trend in college enrollment for high school graduates in 2009, achieving a 50-year historic high for enrollment one year after the start of the Great Recession:

This increase in enrollment was not exclusive to four-year institutions: for-profit postsecondary institutions experienced an increase in enrollment during the Great Recession, while two-year community colleges experienced funding cuts. (Barr & Turner, 2013; Deming, Golden, & Katz, 2012). Figure 1.5 illustrates this for-profit institution enrollment trend, while Figure 1.6 shows the recessionary and post-recessionary enrollment trends between two-year and four-year postsecondary institutions:

Further review of enrollment patterns and projections before and after the Great Recession reveals distinctive trends when disaggregating by sex and race. Figure 1.7 shows that higher education enrollment increased during the Great

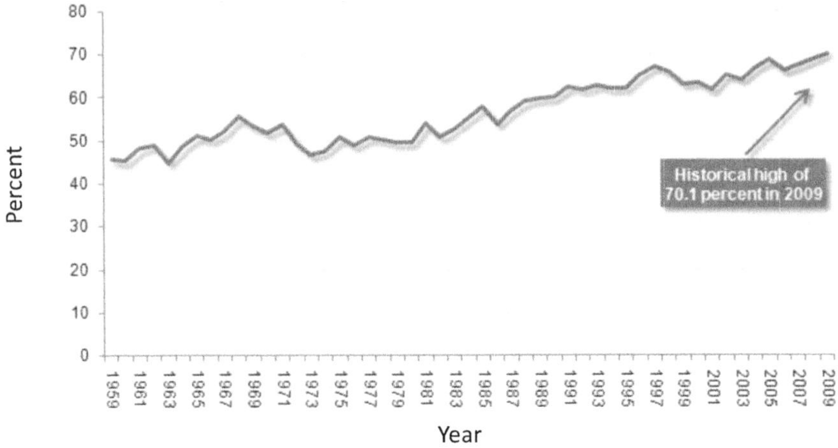

Figure 1.4 College Enrollment Rate of Recent High School Graduates Aged 16–24, October 1959–2009

Source: Bureau of Labor Statistics, U.S. Department of Labor. (2010). The Economics Daily, College enrollment up among 2009 high school grads

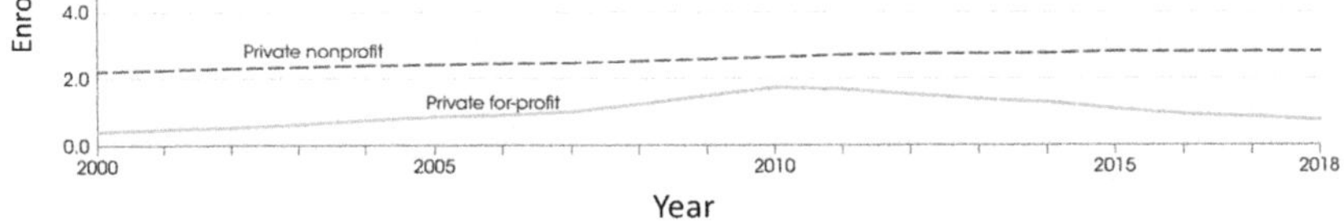

Figure 1.5 Undergraduate Enrollment in Degree-Granting Postsecondary Institutions, by Control of Institution: Fall 2000–2018

Source: Hussar, B., Zhang, J., Hein, S., Wang, K., Roberts, A., Cui, J., Smith, M., Bullock Mann, F., Barmer, A., and Dilig, R. (2020). The Condition of Education 2020 (NCES 2020–144). U.S. Department of Education. Washington, DC: National Center for Education Statistics

Recession for males and females, with female students sustaining a trend of higher postsecondary enrollment relative to males before, during, and after the Great Recession. Enrollment decreased as the Great Recession ended.

Interestingly, Figure 1.8 shows that student increased their postsecondary enrollment during the Great Recession period across various racial/ethnic groups and slowed thereafter. Hispanic[1] student postsecondary enrollment sustained an

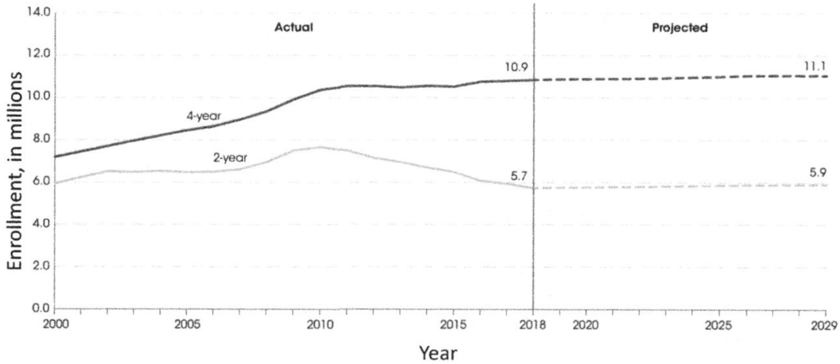

Figure 1.6 Actual and Projected Undergraduate Enrollment in Degree-Granting Postsecondary Institutions, by Level of Institution: Fall 2000 through 2029

Source: Hussar, B., Zhang, J., Hein, S., Wang, K., Roberts, A., Cui, J., Smith, M., Bullock Mann, F., Barmer, A., and Dilig, R. (2020). The Condition of Education 2020 (NCES 2020–144). U.S. Department of Education. Washington, DC: National Center for Education Statistics

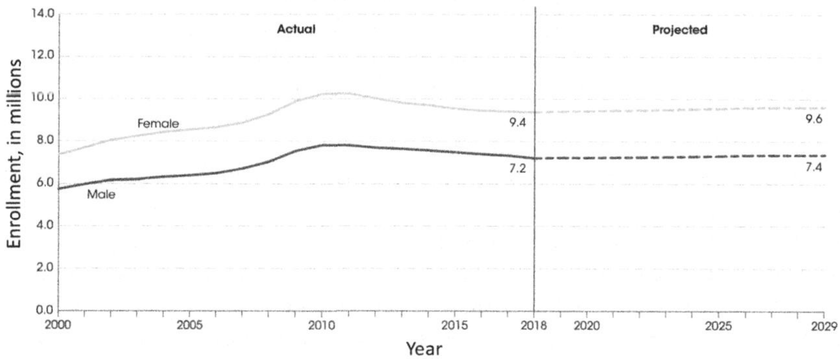

Figure 1.7 Actual and Projected Undergraduate Enrollment in Degree-Granting Postsecondary Institutions, by Sex: Fall 2000–2029

Source: Hussar, B., Zhang, J., Hein, S., Wang, K., Roberts, A., Cui, J., Smith, M., Bullock Mann, F., Barmer, A., and Dilig, R. (2020). The Condition of Education 2020 (NCES 2020–144). U.S. Department of Education. Washington, DC: National Center for Education Statistics

upward trend begun before the Great Recession, continuing during and after the event. Though Black and White student postsecondary enrollment experienced a Great Recession boost, the enrollment momentum went downward after the recession was declared over. The postsecondary enrollment of American Indian/Alaska Natives remained relatively steady both before and during the Great Recession, with a slight downturn after the end of the Great Recession.

U.S. domestic unemployment rates reveal commonalities by race across recessionary periods. Specifically, the Great Recession followed recessionary patterns of disparate effects on racial groups' unemployment rates, with Black/African

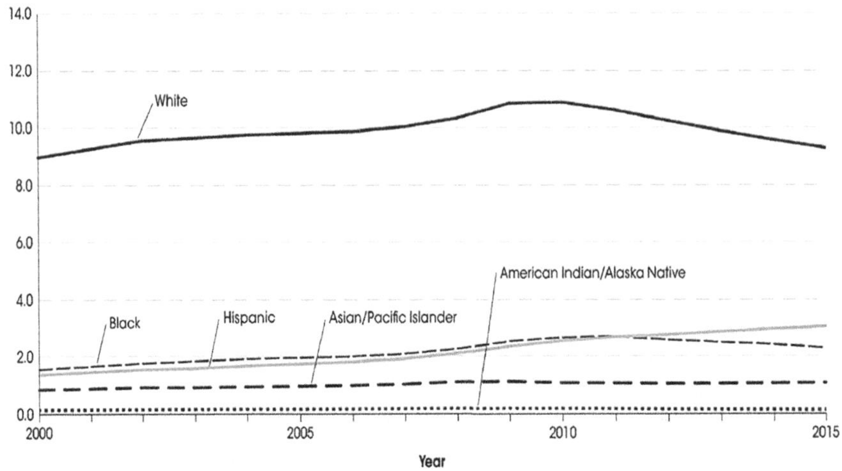

Figure 1.8 Undergraduate Enrollment in Degree-Granting Postsecondary Institutions, by Race/Ethnicity: Fall 2000–2015, Enrollment in Millions

Source: McFarland, J., Hussar, B., de Brey, C., Snyder, T., Wang, X., Wilkinson-Flicker, S., Gebrekristos, S., Zhang, J., Rathbun, A., Barmer, A., Bullock Mann, F., and Hinz, S. (2017). The Condition of Education 2017 (NCES 2017–144). U.S. Department of Education. Washington, DC: National Center for Education Statistics

American persons typically experiencing the highest unemployment rates during and after recessions, Hispanic/Latino persons the second highest, and White persons the lowest recessionary rates of unemployment (see Figure 1.9). The Great Recession was distinctive in the severity of the unemployment status endured by individuals seeking employment, with overall long-term unemployment rates at the highest level compared to previous recessions (see Figure 1.10). This indicates a deeper and longer period of joblessness that created economic pressure among adults that had not been experienced over the previous 10 recessions spanning back to 1948.

Post-Great Recession—Pre-COVID Context and the COVID–19 Global Pandemic

The interim period between the declared ending of the Great Recession and the onset of the COVID-19 pandemic was a time of adjusting to a new normal following the 2007 shock. Using unemployment rates as a proxy, Figure 1.11 illustrates how shock conditions dissipated then emerged again in 2020.

In the lifespan of the young adults under study here, the U.S. experienced a profound cultural shift in its orientation to education learning environments. The precursor conditions prior to the announcement of the global public health emergency found young adults in the U.S. enduring seismic shifts as they advanced through their childhood and adolescent developmental periods. Specifically, the unfathomable reality set in that children, adolescents, and young adults could

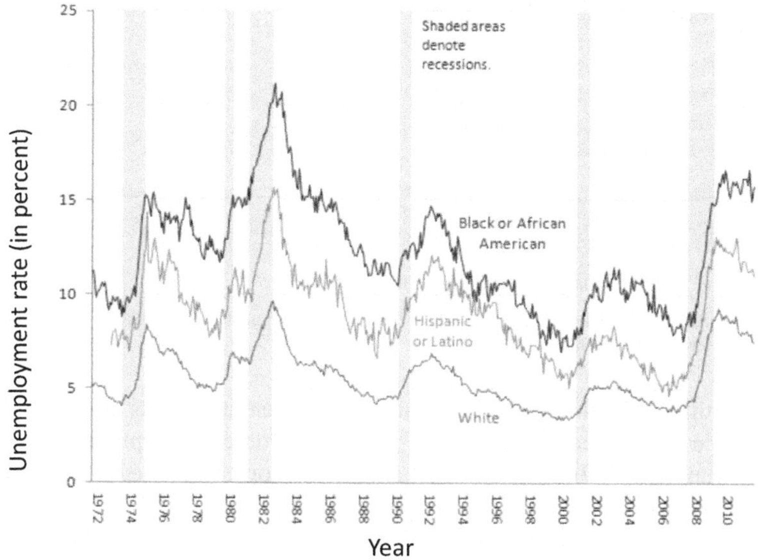

Figure 1.9 Great Recession Unemployment Rate by Race

Source: U.S. Bureau of Labor Statistics. (2012). The recession of 2007–2009. Spotlight on Statistics. U.S. Department of Labor

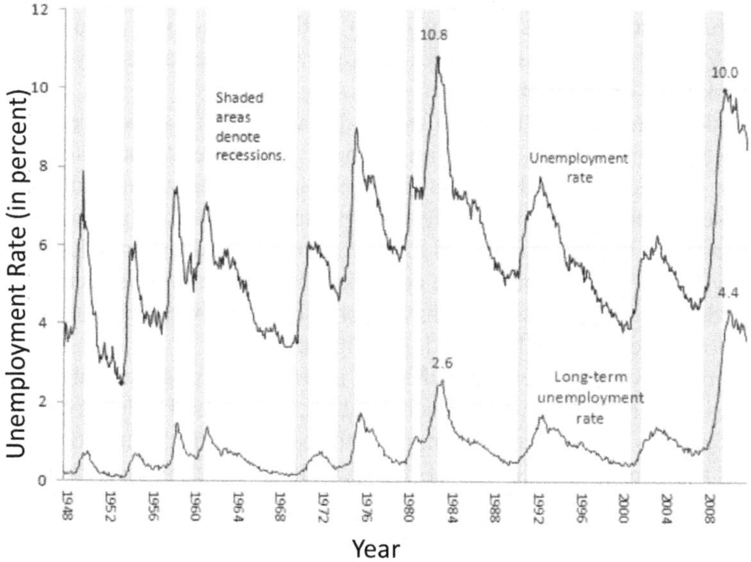

Figure 1.10 Recessionary Unemployment Rates

Source: U.S. Bureau of Labor Statistics. (2012). The recession of 2007–2009. Spotlight on Statistics. U.S. Department of Labor

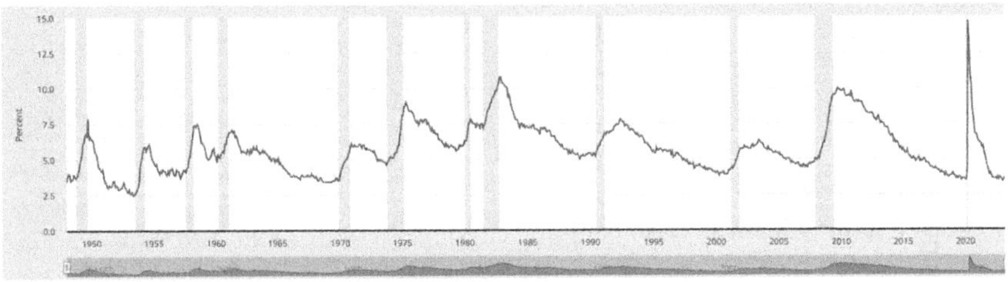

Figure 1.11 Recessionary Unemployment 1948–2021

Source: U.S. Bureau of Labor Statistics. (2023). Unemployment Rate [UNRATE], retrieved from FRED, Federal Reserve Bank of St. Louis

face the threat of lethal violence in their learning environments as school shootings, once considered a rare random event, became commonplace (Grinshteyn & Hemenway, 2019). A reality that might be more associated with attending schools in war-torn locations, schools across the U.S. began to revise school safety preparedness protocols, with active shooter lockdown drills becoming as common as weather-related earthquake and tornado drills. In effect, schools maintained a high state of alertness about the imminent threat of violence with unaddressed repercussions for students' overall mental health and sense of safety (Rygg, 2015). As such, it is important to bear in mind that young adults between the ages of 18 and 20 at the time of the COVID-19 pandemic finished high school conditioned to an awareness of the possibility of imminent threat of bodily harm. This awareness shaped the reality of the school-going population when the COVID-19 pandemic hit in a way that previous generations of young adults had not known or experienced.

An additional stressor for enrolled young adults that gained strength in the Great Recession-COVID-19 interim period was the overall increase in student debt for postsecondary education. The U.S. postsecondary education system is comprised of public and private degree granting institutions that charge tuition for attendance. Payment structures for postsecondary and tertiary education vary globally. The U.S. is among those countries that charge for postsecondary (tertiary) education, and those costs have increased steadily during the post-Great Recession—pre-COVID-19 period (see Figure 1.12).

The cost of college education in the U.S. is financed through a number of mechanisms, including savings, grants, scholarships, and loans. The loans can take the form of parents or caregivers tapping into the equity of their homes or retirement savings to finance the high cost of postsecondary education (see Charles et al., 2015) or students taking out loans. During the Great Recession—COVID-19 interim period, as the cost of postsecondary education steadily increased, particularly at private institutions, student debt followed a similar upward trajectory with student loans alone rising to an historic high of over $1.6 trillion, a tripling of debt at the undergraduate and graduate levels in the period between 2006 and 2020 (Leukhina, 2020; Pyne & Grodsky, 2020).

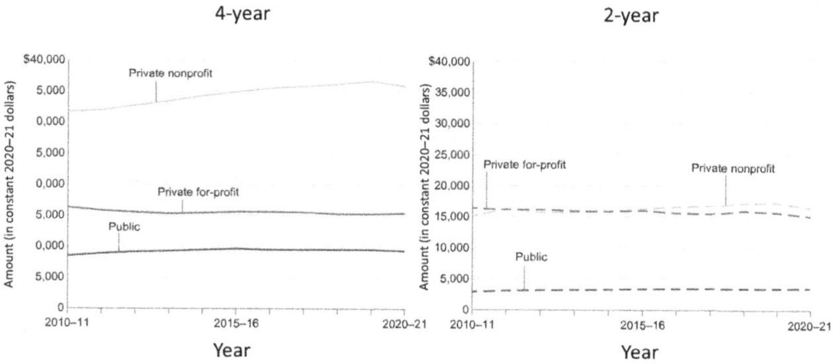

Figure 1.12 Average Annual Undergraduate Tuition and Fees for Full-Time Students at Degree-Granting Postsecondary Institutions, by Level and Control of Institution: Academic Years 2010–2011 through 2020–2021

Source: U.S. Department of Education. Institute of Education Sciences, National Center for Education Statistics

Nonetheless, postsecondary education attainment increased in this interim period. Of particular note is that according to data from NCES, there was an overall increase in the number of degrees conferred that were above the certificate level between the 2010–2011 and 2020–2021 school years, with the following increases at the undergraduate and graduate education levels:

- associate's degrees increase 10 percent (from 943,500 to 1.0 million);
- bachelor's degrees increase 20 percent (from 1.7 million to 2.1 million);
- master's degrees increase 19 percent (from 730,900 to 866,900; and
- doctoral degrees increase 18 percent (from 163,800 to 194,100).

(National Center for Education Statistics, 2023)

The COVID-19 Public Health Emergency

By 2021, one year into the pandemic, the U.S. accounted for 15 percent of the COVID-19 deaths, even though it accounted for less than 5 percent of the global population. The public health emergency precipitated by the virus was declared over on May 11, 2023 (National Center for Immunization and Respiratory Diseases, 2023). This was owed in large part to a slowing down of the spread of infection aided by the arrival of the vaccine, broadened infection-related immunity, and increased availability of therapeutics effective at treating the acute symptoms of the virus. Nonetheless, many suffered from the long-haul after-effects of the virus, with cognitive issues ("brain fog"), depression, posttraumatic stress, and fatigue among complications reported after discharge from COVID-19 intensive care (Guck, Buck, & Lehockey, 2021).

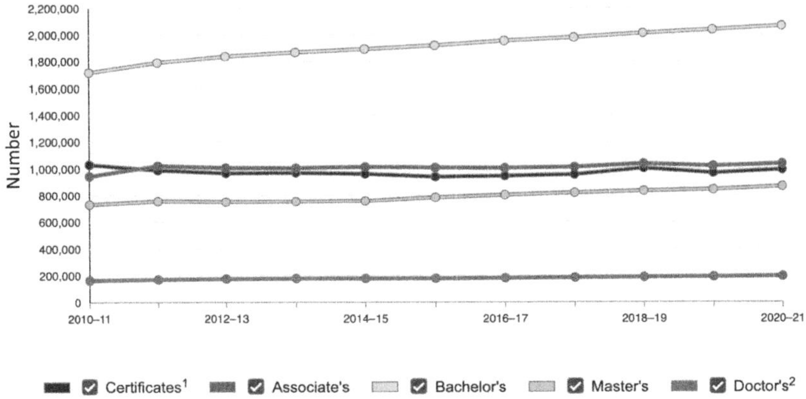

Figure 1.13 Number of Certificates and Degrees Conferred by Postsecondary Institutions, by Award Level: Academic Years 2010–2011 through 2020–2021

Source: National Center for Education Statistics. (2023). Postsecondary Certificates and Degrees Conferred. Condition of Education. U.S. Department of Education, Institute of Education Sciences

Notes: [1] Data are for certificates below the associate's degree level.

[2] Includes Ph.D., Ed.D., and comparable degrees at the doctoral level. Includes most degrees formerly classified as first-professional, such as M.D., D.D.S., and law degrees.

As noted earlier, the infection and mortality rates accelerated an already sobering pattern of lower life expectancy among communities of color in the U.S. (e.g., Millet, Jones, Benkeser, Baral, Mercer, Beyrer, Honermann, Lankiewicz, Mena, Crowley, Sherwood, & Sullivan, 2020; Arias, 2021). These effects were particularly acute in urban areas with high-density living arrangements accompanied by economic and racial segregation. Chicago, a major city in the midwestern state of Illinois in the U.S., highlights the urban COVID effect. Prior to the onset of the COVID-19 global pandemic, Chicago was the site of significant disparities in health outcomes. The term "death gap" was coined by researchers to describe the enduring effects of racial segregation and economic inequality on longevity (Ansell, 2017). A study of average lifespans measured a 30-year difference between the wealthiest, predominantly White zip codes and the poorest Black zip codes (Spoer, Thorpe, Gourevitch, Levine, & Feldman, 2019). In effect, the consequence of living in a poor, predominantly Black zip code in Chicago results in residents dying approximately 30 years earlier than a person who lives in a predominantly White, wealthy zip code. Ansell documents the stark reality of health inequality as "structural violence" that unleashed virulent effects for communities of color in Chicago (Ansell, 2017).

Higher Education in the Age of COVID-19

The impact of the COVID-19 pandemic shock on higher education differed significantly from the previous Great Recession shock. The complete closure of college campuses was an historic first in the U.S. in response to the extreme public health threat that COVID-19 posed. When over 1,000 postsecondary institutions closed for safety concerns, students were sent home *en masse* in what constituted a postsecondary reverse migration, altering not just the physical site of where postsecondary education occurred, but also the psychological orientation to the pursuit of college education, as many students abandoned campus dorms and social milieus to continue their courses remotely.

Emerging research notes the enrollment, learning, and mental health effects of policy changes adopted by many postsecondary institutions in response to COVID-19 closures and restrictions (see Bulman & Fairlie, 2021; Son, Hegde, Smith, Wang, & Sasangohar, 2020). These restrictions were implemented under public health directives across all sectors of the U.S. economy, precipitating an economic recession and housing crisis, compounding the profound negative effects of the virus itself with an accompanying reverse migration for the vast majority of college students as living facilities were closed to avoid COVID-19 transmission. Thus, many students encountered overlapping spheres of risk as they left instituion-based learning environments, moved to online learning environment. Students returned to home environments, and for those whose homes were located in less resourced environments, could me re-entering environments impacted by systemic inequality. These dynamics, then, underscore the importance of acknowledging cumulative, context relevant, and long-term impact of inequality encountered by young adults. When the actual presence of systems of inequality is ignored, overlooked, or simply denied in analyzing the impact of exogenous shocks (see Spencer et al., 2019), its significance is not addressed even though inequality matters profoundly when linked with policies, context features, and everyday practices.

The experience of international students enrolled in higher education merits attention. In 2019, the U.S. led OECD countries and OECD partner countries in its enrollment of international students, with the 977,000 international students accounting for four percent of the overall enrollment in Bachelor's granting programs (OECD, 2021). When broadening the frame to all international students, enrollment reached 1,075,496 in the 2019–2020 school year and by 2020–2021, there was a 15 percent reduction in students enrolled in Bachelor's programs, with incoming freshmen constituting the largest drop at 26 percent (Institute of International Education, 2022). This stands in contrast to the upward trend of international student postsecondary enrollment observed during the period of the Great Recession. (Institute of International Education, 2022). While an overall increase in enrollment accompanied the Great Recession, the period between

2010 and the onset of the COVID-19 pandemic in 2020 reveals an overall increase in degree attainment rates. Figure 1.13 shows the postsecondary degree attainment counts.

A New Lens on an Enduring Phenomenon

The shock events raise new questions about the capacity to sustain the integrity of postsecondary pathways during shock periods. This requires a reexamination of the theoretical and empirical tenets that frame how to understand the effects of shocks on young adulthood relative to individuals' developmental tasks to be mastered (Havighurst, 1953) and the psychological processes involved for meeting the attendant demands as theorized by Erikson and Spencer. It is important to understand how exogenous shocks reorganize the normative assumptions as linked to developmental tasks confronted by all individuals concerning what postsecondary education attainment, as one postsecondary experience pathway, means to young adults as they advance to young adulthood and build or rebuild pathways in the shock aftermath.

A reassessment of this kind is aided by applying a human development perspective to postsecondary outcomes that situate the pursuit of education, work, or other pathways as indelibly situated in the broader context of the young adult developmental stage. A human development perspective, in effect, allows for a more nuanced assessment of how postsecondary experiences facilitate the completion of developmental tasks associated with emergent young adulthood. For racial and ethnic minorities in the U.S., with fewer safety nets to take the risks and make the mistakes associated with this developmental period (see Goff, Jackson, DiLeone, Culotta, & DiTomasso, 2014; Epstein, Blake, & Gonzalez, 2017), the consequences of altered pathways may be more severe as they encounter barriers to access.

Human Capital Theory: Beyond Economic Utility

With education considered a site of skill development, human capital theory's encounter with education measures educational attainment as an index of how a person's function and utility in a society's economy is defined and actualized. Nichols Lodato et al. (2021) consider the implications of human capital theory (Shultz, 1961; Becker, 1964), with its emphasis on the individual utility vis-à-vis the labor market in an economic system. This theory focuses on the functional value of education, enhancing an individual's utility for increasing company value, attaining occupational status, and achieving economic security, particularly in a capitalist economic system. The human developmental considerations are of value insofar as they speak to individual economic utility. This leaves unaddressed the developmental psychological aspects of postsecondary education during young adulthood as an end unto itself, lending individual purpose and meaning to enhance human thriving.

Nichols Lodato et al. posit that an identity-based, context-linked human development perspective addresses the shortcomings of the strict application of a human capital perspective to understand the pursuit of postsecondary education. It is through expanding the theoretical lens to be inclusive of individual developmental, meaning-making processes that open new vistas shaping a novel, shock-sensitive theoretical approach. This approach can account for the effects of an exogenous shock beyond its economic implications, centering the real human consequences of shock disruptions for diverse young adults' developmental experiences.

Approach

This mixed-method study examines what decisions diverse, young adults between 18 and 20 years of age made about their postsecondary education during and after the Great Recession and COVID-19 shocks. The quantitative component utilizes the Panel Study of Income Dynamics Survey (PSID) Transition into Adulthood (TA) Supplement (PSID, 2017) to analyze postsecondary enrollment patterns during and after Great Recession, and how choices about adjustments to education plans possibly speak to underlying changes in the conceptualizations of young adulthood and the transition to adulthood in the U.S. The three research questions that guide the research study are as follows:

- How were the postsecondary education and working patterns for low-income, high-achieving young adults shaped by the Great Recession in comparison to their high-income counterparts?
- How did the Great Recession impact education planning for young adults between the ages of 18 and 20, the key age range for college going?
- Eleven years after the declaration of the close of the Great Recession, which coincides with the COVID-19 pandemic, have there been any changes in the key factors that inform education planning for diverse young adults between the ages of 18 and 20

The results of the quantitative analysis inform a qualitative investigation into young adults' experiences during the period of tumult and disruption caused by the COVID-19 global pandemic. Interviews were conducted with a diverse group of young adults in the Spring of 2021, at the height of the pandemic and in the midst of the broad quarantine shutdowns of schools and businesses. As noted, during this period, the U.S. was also experiencing an associated economic recession alongside global movements toward racial reckoning rooted in the Black Lives Matter movement. Across income and resource levels, both study components provide insights on the developmental implications of diverse young adults' pursuit of education and work plans during shock periods.

Structure of the Book

Following this introduction which details the pertinent scaffolding theories and most significant themes highlighted in this research study, a survey of the literature that frames the investigation is followed by a summary of study methods, presentation of findings, discussion, and conclusion. The review of the relevant literature and theoretical frameworks will inform the three research questions this research project poses. The methods undertaken and findings on the postsecondary statuses (i.e., enrolled in postsecondary education or working) utilize findings from the quantitative study to inform a more in-depth qualitative study of the experiences of 18- to 20-year-olds.

The empirical findings across the two study components motivate the advancement of a new, shock-sensitive theoretical framework, Dynamic Ecological Theory of Identity Development, that provides a strengths-based orientation to identity development among diverse young adults while avoiding the pathologizing difference (for further insights on the theoretical and empirical pitfalls of gap research, see Spencer, Brookins, & Allen, 1985). To avoid the consequences of a strictly binary approach that renders critical developmental aspects of context, culture, and individual meaning making underspecified, this mixed-methods study provides an opportunity to discern the dynamic, strengths-based components of identity development drawn from individual interviews with enrolled students. Specifically, the results from this study, particularly those derived from the qualitative component, offer insights from study participants who, relying upon supports and protective factors, make sense of their risks and challenges as they navigate postsecondary education during shock periods. Across the quantitative and qualitative data, young adults are on the shared road of making a way out of no way during periods where previously-held conventional expectations regarding the stability and reliability of paths were challenged if not done away with altogether. The study findings yield rich insights on how they stay the course and make meaning in the moment to remain true to their education and work goals. They motivate new questions and theoretical considerations for research and policy moving forward.

As a result, in light of the rich racial and ethnic diversity of the U.S. and broader intersectional aspects of identity rooted in gender- and role-based linkages (son, daughter, professional vocation, etc.), for example, a dynamic approach to identity development is undertaken here. This research embraces diversity as a strength, acknowledging systemic phenomena and presenting diversity to highlight dimensions of humanity rather than pathologizing difference to privilege one group's attainment at the expense of the consideration of another's intrinsic humanity.

Getting Our Bearings

The study of postsecondary education is an interdisciplinary enterprise, as the fields of education, psychology, sociology, and economics are among the disciplines in the social sciences that explore the distinctive social scientific facets of this endeavor. For this reason, before delving into the study design and findings, it is useful to review the key theoretical frameworks and applied research that informs how postsecondary education, identity, and shocks have been engaged across the social sciences.

Note

1 The terms "Hispanic" and "Latinx" and "Latino" are used in this book in accordance with the terms term utilized in the national datasets analyzed in the study, literature sources and participant self-identification. It is important to note that these broad racial/ethnic categories encompass varied national and cultural origins and historic trajectories.

References

Andrasfay, T., & Goldman, N. (2021). Reductions in 2020 US life expectancy due to COVID-19 and the disproportionate impact on the Black and Latino populations. *Proceedings of the National Academy of Sciences of the United States of America, 118*(5). https://doi.org.proxy.uchicago.edu/10.1073/pnas.2014746118.

Ansell, D. A. (2017). *The death gap: How inequality kills*. Chicago: University of Chicago Press.

Arias, E., Tejada-Vera, B., Ahmad, F., & Kochanek, K. D. (2021). *Provisional life expectancy estimates for 2020. Vital statistics rapid release; No 15*. Hyattsville, MD: National Center for Health Statistics. https://dx.doi.org/10.15620/cdc:107201.

Bailey, M. J., & Dynarski, S. M. (2011). Gains and gaps: Changing inequality in US college entry and completion (No. w17633). National Bureau of Economic Research.

Barr, A., & Turner, S. E. (2013). Expanding enrollments and contracting state budgets: The effect of the great recession on higher education. *The ANNALS of the American Academy of Political and Social Science, 650*(1), 168–193.

Becker, G. S. (1964). *Human capital: A theoretical and empirical analysis, with special reference to education by Gary S. Becker*. London: National Bureau of Economic Research.

Billari, F. C., & Liefbroer, A. C. (2010). Towards a new pattern of transition to adulthood? *Advances in Life Course Research, 15*(2), 59–75. https://doi.org.proxy.uchicago.edu/10.1016/j.alcr.2010.10.003.

Bulman, G., & Fairlie, R. W. (2021). *The impact of COVID-19 on community college enrollment and student success: Evidence from California administrative data*. Retrieved from https://doi.org.proxy.uchicago.edu/http://www.nber.org/papers/w28715.pdf.

Bureau of Labor Statistics, U.S. Department of Labor. (2010). The Economics Daily, College enrollment up among 2009 high school grads.

Centers for Disease Control and Prevention. (2023). *COVID data tracker*. Atlanta, GA: U.S. Department of Health and Human Services. Retrieved from https://covid.cdc.gov/covid-data-tracker

Charles, K. K., Hurst, E., & Notowidigdo, M. J. (2015). Housing booms and busts, labor market opportunities, and college attendance (NBER Working Paper No. 21587, JEL No. E24), September, pp. I21, J24.

Chetty, R., Hendren, N., Kline, P., Saez, E., & Turner, N. (2014). Is the United States still a land of opportunity? Recent trends in intergenerational mobility. *American Economic Review, 104*(5), 141–147.

Deming, D., Goldin, C., & Katz, L. (2012). The for-profit postsecondary school sector: Nimble critters or agile predators? *The Journal of Economic Perspectives*, *26*(1), 139–164.

Dettling, L. J., Hsu, J. W., & Llanes, E. (2018). *A wealthless recovery? Asset ownership and the uneven recovery from the Great Recession* (FEDS Notes). Washington, DC: Board of Governors of the Federal Reserve System. https://doi.org/10.17016/2380-7172.2249.

Elsby, M. W., Hobijn, B., & Sahin, A. (2010). The labor market in the great recession (Working Paper 15979). Retrieved from http://www.nber.org/papers/w15979.

Epstein, R., Blake, J., & Gonzalez, T. (2017). *Girlhood interrupted: The erasure of Black girls' childhood*. Washington, DC: Georgetown Law Center on Poverty and Inequality. Retrieved from https://www.blendedandblack.com/wp-content/uploads/2017/08/girlhood-interrupted.pdf.

Erikson, E. H. (1950). *Childhood in society*. New York: Norton.

Erikson, E. H. (1968). *Identity: Youth and crisis*. New York: Norton and Company.

Faust J. S., Lin, Z., & del Rio, C. (2020). Comparison of estimated excess deaths in New York City during the COVID-19 and 1918 influenza pandemics. *JAMA New Open*, *3*(8), e2017527. https://doi.org/10.1001/jamanetworkopen.2020.17527.

Goff, P. A., Jackson, M. C., Di Leone, B. A. L., Culotta, C. M., & Di Tomasso, N. A. (2014). The essence of innocence: Consequences of dehumanizing Black children. *Journal of Personality and Social Psychology*, *106*, 526–545. https://doi.org/10.1037/a0035663.

Gould Ellen, I., & Dastrup, S. (2012). *Housing and the Great Recession*. Stanford, CA: Stanford Center on Poverty and Inequality.

Grinshteyn, E., & Hemenway, D. (2019). Violent death rates in the US compared to those of the other high-income countries, 2015. *Preventive Medicine*, *123*, 20–26.

Guck, A. J., Buck, K., & Lehockey, K. (2021). Psychological complications of COVID-19 following hospitalization and ICU discharge: Recommendations for treatment. *Professional Psychology: Research and Practice*. https://doi.org.proxy.uchicago.edu/10.1037/pro0000402

Havighurst, R. J. (1953). *Human development and education*. New York: McKay.

Hussar, B., Zhang, J., Hein, S., Wang, K., Roberts, A., Cui, J., Smith, M., Bullock Mann, F., Barmer, A., and Dilig, R. (2020). The Condition of Education 2020 (NCES 2020–144). U.S. Department of Education. Washington, DC: National Center for Education Statistics.

Institute of International Education. (2022). International students by academic level, 1999/00–2021/22. *Open Doors Report on International Educational Exchange*. Retrieved from http//www.opendoorsdata.org.

Juárez, F., & Gayet, C. (2014). Transitions to adulthood in developing countries. *Annual Review of Sociology*, *40*, 521–538. https://doi.org.proxy.uchicago.edu/10.1146/annurev-soc-052914-085540.

Leukhina, O. (2020, January 14). On the economy blog: Rising student debt and the great recession. *Federal Reserve Bank of St. Louis*. Retrieved from https://www.stlouisfed.org/en/on-the-economy/2020/january/rising-student-debt-great-recession.

Lloyd, C. B., & National Research Council (U.S.). (2005). *Growing up global: The changing transitions to adulthood in developing countries*. London: National Academies Press.

Long, B. T. (2014). The financial crisis and college enrollment: How have students and their families responded? In J. R. Brown & C. M. Hoxby (Eds.), *How the financial crisis and great recession affected higher education*. Chicago: The University of Chicago Press.

Long, B. T., & Adukia, A. (2009). *The impact of the financial crisis on tertiary education worldwide: A pilot study (Draft Paper)*. Cambridge, MA: Harvard Graduation School of Education.

McFarland, J., Hussar, B., de Brey, C., Snyder, T., Wang, X., Wilkinson-Flicker, S., Gebrekristos, S., Zhang, J., Rathbun, A., Barmer, A., Bullock Mann, F., and Hinz, S. (2017). *The Condition of Education 2017 (NCES 2017–144)*. U.S. Department of Education. Washington, DC: National Center for Education Statistics.

Millett, G. A., Jones, A. T., Benkeser, D., Baral, S., Mercer, L., Beyrer, C., Honermann, B., Lankiewicz, E., Mena, L., Crowley, J. S., Sherwood, J., & Sullivan, P. (2020). Assessing differential impacts of COVID-19 on black communities. *Annals of Epidemiology*. https://doi.org.proxy.uchicago.edu/10.1016/j.annepidem.2020.05.003.

Montgomery, M. J., & Côte, J. E. (2003). College as a transition to adulthood. In G. R. Adams & M. Berzonsky (Eds.) *Blackwell handbook of adolescence*. John Wiley & Sons.

National Center for Immunization and Respiratory Diseases (NCIRD), Division of Viral Diseases. (2022). *Long COVID or post-COVID conditions*. Retrieved from https://www.cdc.gov/coronavirus/2019-ncov/long-term-effects/index.html.

National Center for Immunization and Respiratory Diseases (NCIRD), Division of Viral Diseases. (2023). End of the federal COVID-19 Public Health Emergency (PHE) declaration. *Center for Disease Control and Prevention*. Retrieved from https://www.cdc.gov/coronavirus/2019-ncov/your-health/end-of-phe.html.

National Center for Education Statistics. (2023). Postsecondary certificates and degrees conferred. *Condition of Education. U.S. Department of Education, Institute of Education Sciences*. Retrieved from https://nces.ed.gov/programs/coe/indicator/cts.

Neugarten, B. L., & Datan, N. (1973). Sociological perspectives on the life cycle. In *Life-span developmental psychology* (pp. 53–69). Academic Press.

Neugarten, B. L. (1976). Adaptation and the life cycle. *The counseling psychologist*, *6*(1), 16–20.

Nichols Lodato, B., Hall, J., & Spencer, M. (2021). Vulnerability and resiliency implications of human capital and linked inequality presence denial perspectives: Acknowledging Zigler's contributions to child well-being. *Development and Psychopathology*, 1–16. https://doi.org/10.1017/S0954579420001893.

OECD. (2021). What is the profile of internationally mobile students? In *Education at a glance 2021: OECD indicators*. Paris: OECD Publishing. https://doi.org/10.1787/5a49e448-en.

PSID Main Interview User Manual: Release (2017). *Institute for social research*. Ann Arbor, MI: University of Michigan.

Pyne, J., & Grodsky, E. (2020). Inequality and opportunity in a perfect storm of graduate student debt. *Sociology of Education*, *93*(1), 20–39. https://doi.org/10.1177/0038040719876245.

Rodriguez-Diaz, C. E., Guilamo-Ramos, V., Mena, L., Hall, E., Honermann, B., Crowley, J. S., Baral, S., Prado, G. J., Marzan-Rodriguez, M., Beyrer, C., Sullivan, P. S., & Millett, G. A. (2020). Risk for COVID-19 infection and death among Latinos in the United States: Examining heterogeneity in transmission dynamics. *Annals of Epidemiology*, *52*, 46–53. https://doi.org.proxy.uchicago.edu/10.1016/j.annepidem.2020.07.007.

Rygg, L. (2015). School shooting simulations: At what point does preparation become more harmful than helpful. *Children's Legal Rights Journal*, *35*, 215.

Schultz, T. W. (1961). Investment in human capital. *American Economic Review*, *51*(1), 1.

Son, C., Hegde, S., Smith, A., Wang, X., & Sasangohar, F. (2020). Effects of COVID-19 on college students' mental health in the United States: Interview survey study. *Journal of Medical Internet Research*, *22*(9), e21279. https://doi.org/10.2196/21279.

Spencer, M. B. (2006). Phenomenology and ecological systems theory: Development of diverse groups. In R. M. Lerner & W. Damon (Eds.), *Handbook of child psychology, vol. 1: Theoretical models of human development*, 6th ed. (pp. 829–893). New York: Wiley Publishers.

Spencer, M. B., Brookins, G. K., & Allen, W. R. (Eds.). (1985). *Beginnings: The social and affective development of black children*. London: Lawrence Erlbaum Associates, Inc.

Spoer, B., Thorpe, L., Gourevitch, M., Levine, S., & Feldman, J. (2019). Census tract-level association between racial composition and life expectancy among 492 large cities in the United States. *Annals of Epidemiology*, *40*, 38.

Standing, G. (2011). *The precariat: The new dangerous class* (p. 208). London: Bloomsbury Academic.

U.S. Bureau of Labor Statistics. (2012). The recession of 2007–2009. *Spotlight on Statistics*. U.S. Department of Labor.

U.S. Bureau of Labor Statistics. (2023). Unemployment Rate [UNRATE], retrieved from FRED, Federal Reserve Bank of St. Louis.

U.S. Census Bureau (2015). 2010–2014 American Community Survey 5-year estimates.

U.S. Department of Education. Institute of Education Sciences, National Center for Education Statistics.

United States Government Accountability Office. (2022). Student loans: Education has increased federal cost estimates of direct loans by billions due to programmatic and other changes (GAO-22-105365). Report to Congressional Requesters.

United Nations Educational, Scientific and Cultural Organization (UNESCO) Institute for Statistics. (2020). *Tertiary enrollment data as of September 2020*.

The University of Chicago Data Science Initiative. (2022). Digital divide: Data highlights internetinequities in Chicago. The University of Chicago. Retrieved from https://datascience.uchicago.edu/news/digital-divide-data-highlights-internet-inequities-in-chicago/.

The World Bank. (2023). *Life expectancy at birth, total (years)*. Retrieved from https://data.worldbank.org/indicator/SP.DYN.LE00.IN.

World Health Organization. (2021). *Adolescent health*. Retrieved from https://covid19.who.int.

World Health Organization. (2023). *WHO coronavirus (COVID-19) dashboard*.

Wright, D. A., Ramdin, G., & Vásquez-Colina, M. D. (2013). The effects of four decades of recession on higher education enrollments in the United States. *Universal Journal of Educational Research*, *1*(3), 154–164. Retrieved from http://search.ebscohost.com.proxy.uchicago.edu/login.aspx?direct=true&db=eric&AN=EJ1053879&site=eds-live&scope=site.

Yancy, C. W. (2020). COVID-19 and African Americans. *Journal of the American Medical Association*, *323*(19), 1891–1892. https://doi.org/10.1001/jama.2020.6548.

2 The Role of Education in Society

In examining the role of education in the life course, it is useful to consider key theoretical frameworks across the social sciences that speak to the role of education in a society. In particular, postsecondary education is a critical marker for designating readiness and preparation to assume an occupation as an adult as well as citizenship responsibilities, more generally.

The introduction presented key conceptual constructs and a review of the unique attributes of the Great Recession and COVID-19 as exogenous shocks and established the concept of young adulthood as a psychosocial developmental stage. Additionally, patterns of inequality and discriminatory practices operating in developmental contexts can produce particularly acute negative effects. Put another way, when considering human development broadly, it is important to acknowledge that not all starts are homogenous, and young adult pathways vary. To ascertain the tensions between a human development and human capital perspective on the role and purpose of education vis-à-vis the individual necessitates accounting for phenomenologically driven identity development processes at work as postsecondary education is pursued.

This chapter provides overview of how different theoretical perspectives have engaged the role of education in a society and the market-based framing of the purpose of education as a site for skill development. It then reviews key theorizing around the concept of capital and the effect of systemic inequality, with acknowledgement of the legal framework that altered the notion of who is entitled to access education as a fundamental right.

The Role of Education in Society

The education system in the U.S. is a misnomer, as it is not a singular system centrally administered, but rather it is comprised of over 120,000 elementary and secondary schools and over 3,500 public and private postsecondary institutions (NCES, 2022). Nonetheless, the term system is useful to describe the singular endeavor to develop the intellectual, social, and emotional skills of youths

DOI: 10.4324/9781003404842-2

and young adults. The form and structure of the institutions and the governing frameworks have evolved over time. Noteworthy legal decisions, such as Brown v. Board of Education, which removed the legal enforcement of "separate but equal" doctrine, ending government-sanctioned racially segregated schools in the U.S., and the American with Disabilities Act that guaranteed rights of access to students with needs, served to expand access to education for all citizens. While the legal framework permitting broader access to education in the mid-20th century moved toward access and equity, the latter stages of the century through the COVID-19 pandemic experienced a disturbing regression toward racial and ethnic segregation of schools as the U.S. became increasingly diverse (United States General Accountability Office, 2022). At the center of these debates and trends was the discernment of the role of education in U.S. society as both a right and a developmental imperative.

Here, it is useful to highlight the foundational perspective of education in the U.S. advanced by John Dewey in his book, *School and Society* (1915). In it, he set forth key principles considered central to the purpose of education in a rapidly changing society. Linking the function of education to market needs, Dewey argued that an education system was critical for developing productive workers and ultimately preparing individuals to assume the responsibilities of citizenship in a society undergoing a technological revolution. Students would emerge from their educational training poised to take their place in a rapidly advancing society undergoing a technological revolution in the early 20th century (Dewey, 1915). This idea continues to shape how education is viewed in the U.S. to this day, with additional ideas regarding education's function engaged from other vantage points toward distinctive purposes. For example, while Dewey held primary interest in the development of citizens in a democratic society, Schultz, in describing investment in human capital, highlighted the significant returns, i.e., higher earnings, for workers who pursue additional education (Schultz, 1961). Becker's work further expanded the notion of human capital, in which citizens' value is viewed through their utility to the market and the generation of profits, which in turn can improve their overall well-being through improving their skills (Becker, 1964).

The notion of human capital took hold in economics and drew the attention of sociologists seeking to further theorize on the sociological implications of education. Specifically, Bourdieu sought to bridge the sociological and economic perspectives by providing insights on the various forms of capital, identifying other categories of capital, such as embodied capital and cultural capital, that can accrue to an individual and impact their success in a broader labor market (Bourdieu, 1986). Coleman's theory of social capital, on the other hand, sought to repair deficiencies he observed in sociology's conceptualization of the role of social systems, which deprived individuals of an "engine of action," and economics' theorizing about human capital, which assumed unrealistically atomistic motivating factors governing individual behavior (Coleman, 1988).

These theories provide frameworks to understand education's role in society, but this work also necessitates the consideration of the context in which educational pursuits and development occur. Notably, the emphasis on the value of an education for enhancing human capital, which has become more dominant throughout the social sciences (for example, see Tan, 2014 for a discussion of human capital theory in education research), prioritizes a utilitarian orientation to education, centering the importance of human beings as rational actors in a market economy. However, human beings living in a diverse, dynamic society undertake their education in contexts that vary and afford different types of resources to support their growth and development. Hence, the accommodation of a developmental approach informed by an awareness of the risks, challenges, and supports found in living environments can enrich any investigation into educational experiences.

Inequality Presence Denial and Unequal Spaces. In their article documenting the contribution of Dr. Edward Zigler, founder of Head Start, Nichols Lodato, Hall, and Spencer (2021) acknowledge the role of inequality in the U.S. and its impact on developmental contexts. In particular, diverse youths residing in under-resourced contexts experience exacerbated risks and challenges by virtue of where they live. The authors state that policies that have resulted in spatial inequality and discriminatory housing practices compound risk factors that shape the developmental trajectories of diverse youths. Exposure to under-resourced environments raises the stakes for diverse youths to find sufficient supports to cultivate coping mechanisms necessary for positive identity development. The authors point to research by Allard (2009) and Rothstein (2017) that indicates the nature and categories of discriminatory practices. Rothstein notes that decades of housing discrimination enforced by federal, state, and local policies engrained segregated housing patterns that became linked to segregated schools as families were forced "to move to segregated neighborhoods if they wanted education for their children" (Rothstein, 2017, p. 122). Wilson and Taub note the importance of examining the dynamics of neighborhood contexts and the influence on outcomes (Wilson & Taub, 2006). In his study of the social safety net, Scott Allard documented the effects of spatial inequality (Allard, 2009). He notes that sources of supports forming the fabric of social safety nets in a community are not optimally placed in high poverty areas where the need is the greatest. Residents from communities of color are disproportionately represented in these areas that lack resources. Allard's analysis of three large urban areas indicates that "mismatches in the spatial distribution of service providers can help to explain why many social programs experience low take-up rates, high rates of attrition, and less than optimal outcomes" (Allard, 2009, p. 86).

Nichols Lodato et al. continue that since the launch of the War on Poverty in 1965, overall poverty has decreased while inequality has expanded as the population in the U.S. has grown more diverse. They point to Reardon's macroanalysis of education longitudinal data that revealed the critical truth of the effects of inequality—that is, it is far reaching and can undermine progress for U.S. society overall. He notes the failure associated with not interrogating the role of rising inequality as a key driver in education outcomes:

> [M]uch of our public conversation about education is focused on the wrong culprits: we blame failing schools and the behavior of the poor for trends that are really the result of deepening income inequality and the behavior of the rich.
>
> (Reardon, 4/27/13, New York Times)

These documented patterns of inequality in the U.S. that are present in various sectors of society, notably housing, education, and the judicial system, play out against a backdrop of growing negative effects of health outcomes for people of color. These negative effects are apparent in unequivocal terms, as noted by COVID-19 infection and mortality statistics, as cited in Chapter 1.

As noted earlier, theories that do not account for the role of inequality and endemic systemic racial bias, with their overlapping and disparate effects, can find remedy in the conceptual shortfalls in their perspectives by utilizing a human development lens to aid in understanding how exogenous shocks impact identity development trajectories over the life course. Indeed, Nichols Lodato et al. (2021) note the interconnected, identity-linked nature of social inequality as it impacts the cultivation of coping processes that undergird positive identity development:

> [C]oping processes experienced in context are linked to identity. This is particularly important when considering that societal inequalities are often based upon identity. Thus, social inequality itself, then, provides a shared context for determining coping responses, and this very process becomes part of identity formation. When certain social identities are more likely to be pathologized, victimized, and excluded, then shared coping strategies are especially important for determining best practices as supports.
>
> (Nichols Lodato et al., 2021, p. 3)

However, these adverse effects do not have to endure. Glen Elder's landmark research in the book *Children of the Great Depression* (Elder, 1999), which founded the field of life course research, examines the longitudinal effects of the Great Depression with the family's response to the shocks as the primary unit of analysis for understanding the effects of a shock on life outcomes across a range of domains, including education, work, and family formation. The significance of Elder's pre-eminent work opened up a rich avenue of investigation regarding the life course implications of shocks that have economic repercussions. As Elder followed a sample of youths from Oakland, California, into early adulthood.

Interestingly, he notes that the Great Depression's negative impacts on social and family structures did not endure into adulthood by mid-life, thus not engendering a "blighted generation" as anticipated. He detailed descriptions of the resources present in the developmental contexts (e.g., schools that focused on equalizing access to enrichment activities for all students regardless of income). Not pointing to a single formula, he underscores the importance of assessing the context to ascertain the aspects of lived environments that produce successful adaptation. Elder notes:

> To understand why some persons successfully adapt to challenging situations and others do not requires knowledge of their resources and motivation, the support provided by the family and larger environment, and characteristics of the event or situation itself.
>
> (Elder, 1999, p. 35)

Compounding Inequality

Since the Great Recession ended and the announcement of the COVID-19 public health emergency, profound inequality has emerged in the U.S. (Nau, 2016), a society that holds the pursuit of happiness and equality as principles enshrined in the country's founding documents. Whether formally acknowledged or not, empirical research points to the expansion and deepening of economic inequality having implications for intergenerational mobility. Chetty, Hendren, Kline, Saez, and Turner (2014) determined that intergenerational mobility was relatively stable even in the wake of rising economic inequality after the Great Recession. However, subsequent research has found that for students designated having low incomes in particular, there is variance in postsecondary institutions' ability to produce successful outcomes, thereby negatively impacting intergenerational upward mobility for this group (Chetty, Friedman, Saez, Turner, & Yagan, 2017). In their examination of outcomes between 2000 and 2011 for cohorts of persons born between 1980 and 1991, Chetty et al. (2017) stated the following: "[i]n sum, the colleges that offered many low-income children pathways to upward mobility (in an accounting sense) are becoming less accessible to them, potentially reducing the scope for higher education to foster intergenerational mobility" (Chetty et al., 2017, p. 41). When viewed through a human developmental lens, the emergence of the COVID-19 pandemic heightened the risks faced by young adults, ex- acerbating the preexisting precarity brought about by economic instability and inequality.

For sure, inequality merits interrogation as a dynamic factor in developmental contexts given its effects on life course outcomes; this is the case whether its presence and salience are formally acknowledged or denied given normal human development processes (see Spencer et al., 2019). Nichols Lodato et al. (2021) underscore the lack of consideration of the pernicious effects of inequality on human development. Certainly, the work of economists such as Chetty (*Ibid.*) and Piketty (2015) shows that inequality is an empirically proven phenomenon with direct impacts on life outcomes of individuals. Indeed, the fact that inequality is a measurable variable creates the conceptual space in which it is possible to account for its effect on the systems and networks where individuals reside and development. One example, Chetty's Opportunity Atlas (2018) allows for incorporating inequality effects by tracing the intergenerational consequences of growing up in lower versus higher-resourced environments. In sum:

> [A]cknowledging that inequality exists as an empirical fact then necessitates consideration of the violent effects of poverty on development for all children, with particular virulent effects on youths of color who are also impacted by the heightened, morbid levels of risks owed to discriminatory practices in the education, health, and judicial systems in the United States.
>
> (Nichols Lodato et al., 2021, p. 13)

The emergence of the global pandemic and societal reckonings with racial injustice and broad inequality emphasized the need to change pre-existing inequitable patterns and norms of inclusion and access to meet basic needs that undergird notions of a functioning society and support the nurturing of youths' development (Nichols Lodato et al., 2021). These conditions give rise to high levels of "morbid risk" particularly for communities of color, with the need to better understand how to provide context-relevant, culturally responsive (Spencer, 1999) resources to marshal appropriate supports.

Overall, these theoretical perspectives do not address the key question of how societal shifts emanating from the exogenous shocks shape young adults' conceptualization of (i.e., meaning making) and accessibility to traditional (i.e., work, education) and emerging pathways that mold the transition to adulthood. As observed in Silva's work on traditional and evolving narratives of emerging adulthood (Silva, 2012), shock events expand understanding of how the pursuit of education and work during early adulthood adapts and changes in response to transformative events that occur in Bronfenbrenner's chronosystem (see Chapter 3). Key to engaging this open question is obtaining a better grasp of the interface between the contextual assumptions and the realities of how young adults make meaning of risks and challenges, cope with the risks by drawing upon resources present and accessed as supports, and define young adulthood paths to subsequently actualize their ambitions in education and work. This study addresses this theoretical gap by investigating the effects of shocks on diverse young adults' postsecondary experiences in education and work, and how those experiences informed their young adulthood identity development, thereby setting the direction of their life course.

References

Allard, S. W. (2009). *Out of reach: Place, poverty, and the New American welfare state*. New Haven, CT: Yale University Press.

Becker, G. S. (1964). *Human capital: A theoretical and empirical analysis, with special reference to education/by Gary S. Becker*. London: National Bureau of Economic Research.

Bourdieu, P. (1986). Forms of capital. In J. Richardson (Ed.), *Handbook of theory and research for the sociology of education*. New York: Greenwood Press.

Chetty, R., Friedman, J. N., Hendren, N., Jones, M. R., & Porter, S. R. (2018). The opportunity atlas: Mapping the childhood roots of social mobility (No. w25147). National Bureau of Economic Research.

Chetty, R., Friedman, J. N., Saez, E., Turner, N., & Yagan, D. (2017). Mobility report cards: The role of colleges in intergenerational mobility (Working Paper Series).

Chetty, R., Hendren, N., Kline, P., Saez, E., & Turner, N. (2014). Is the United States still a land of opportunity? Recent trends in intergenerational mobility. *The American Economic Review*, *104*(5), 141–147. https://doi.org.proxy.uchicago.edu/10.1257/aer.104.5.141.

Coleman, J. (1988). Social capital in the creation of human capital. *American Journal of Sociology*, *94*, S95–S120.

Dewey, J. (1915). *School and society*. Chicago: The University of Chicago Press.

Elder, G. H. J., Bronfenbrenner, U., & Clausen, J. A. (1999). *Children of the great depression: Social change in life experience* (25th Anniversary ed.). Boulder, CO: Westview Press.

Innovating resilience promotion: Integrating cultural practices, social ecologies and development-sensitive conceptual strategies for advancing child well-being. (2019). In D. A. Henry, E. Votruba-Drzal & P. Miller (Eds.), *Advances in child development and behavior: Child development at the intersection of race and SES*, Vol. 57. Elsevier Academic Press.

National Center for Education Statistics. (2022). Characteristics of degree-granting postsecondary institutions. *Condition of Education. U.S. Department of Education, Institute of Education Sciences*. Retrieved June 29, 2023, from https://nces.ed.gov/programs/coe/indicator/csa.

National Center for Education Statistics. (2023). Digest of education statistics, 2022. U.S. Department of Education.

Nau, M. D. (2016). Whose Financial Crisis? How the Great Recession Reshaped Economic Instability and Inequality in the US (Doctoral dissertation, The Ohio State University).

Nichols Lodato, B., Hall, J., & Spencer, M. (2021). Vulnerability and resiliency implications of human capital and linked inequality presence denial perspectives: Acknowledging Zigler's contributions to child well-being. *Development and Psychopathology*, 1–16. https://doi.org/10.1017/S0954579420001893

Piketty, T. (2015). *The economics of inequality*. Cambridge, MA: The Belknap Press of Harvard University Press.

Rothstein, R. (2017). *The color of law: A forgotten history of how our government segregated America*. New York: Liveright Publishing Corporation.

Schultz, T. W. (1961). Investment in human capital. *American Economic Review*, *51*(1), 1.

Silva, J. M. (2012). Constructing adulthood in an age of uncertainty. *American Sociological Review*, *77*(4), 505–522.

Spencer, M. B. (1999). Social and cultural influences on school adjustment: The application of an identity-focused cultural ecological perspective. *Educational Psychologist*, *34*(1), 43–57.

Tan, E. (2014). Human capital theory: A holistic criticism. *Review of Educational Research, 84*, 411–445. https://doi.org/10.3102/0034654314532696.

U.S. Department of Education, National Center for Education Statistics, Integrated Postsecondary Education Data System (IPEDS), Winter 2020–21, Admissions component. See Digest of Education Statistics 2021, table 305.40.

United States Government Accountability Office. (2022). K-12 Education: Student population has significantly diversified, but many schools remain divided along racial, ethnic, and economic lines. *Report to the Chairman, Committee on Education and Labor, House of Representatives*.

Wilson, W. J., & Taub, R. P. (2006). *There goes the neighborhood: Racial, ethnic, and class tensions in four Chicago neighborhoods and their meaning for America*. New York: Alfred A. Knopf.

3 Identity Development and Postsecondary Education

The concepts of context and meaning making are critical to the application of a human development perspective in the study of shocks' impact on education experiences and linkages to identity development processes. Urie Bronfenbrenner's Ecological Systems Theory and Margaret Beale Spencer's Phenomenological Variant of Ecological Systems Theory (PVEST) are essential to capturing the multilayered interconnected nature of context and identity development. Further, linking conceptual frameworks, Bronfenbrenner highlights Glen Elder's *Children of the Great Depression* (1999) as an exemplar of a person-process-context approach to understanding contextual dimensions of development. The nature and timing of young adult milestone attainment as an outcomes-based framing are thrown up in the air during shock periods, introducing a kind of limbo in which chronological age-linked milestones are no longer in sync with expected sequence of outcomes. With the connection established between context and the presence of risk and challenges as contributing dynamics in identity development for diverse youths, the previous chapter reviewed literature exploring the effect of exogenous shocks which have ramifications over the life course. This chapter delves into the literature that frames the study of shock events on postsecondary education experiences and plans, centered around an understanding of adolescent and young adult identity development, postsecondary pathways and context.

Context and Phenomenological Processes in Identity Development

Human development theoretical frameworks that address context and vulnerability as critical levers informing advancement through life stages, as conceptualized by Erikson (1950, 1968), prove useful for understanding the identity development of diverse young adults (18–20) as they pursue education and work. They provide essential epistemological support for employing the comparative human development theoretical framing that drives this work. As such, Urie Bronfenbrenner's Ecological Systems Theory (Bronfenbrenner, 1986, 1993) and Margaret Beale Spencer's Phenomenological Variant of Ecological Systems Theory (EST; Bronfenbrenner, 1986, 1993) (PVEST: Spencer, 1995, 2006, 2008; Spencer, Dupree, & Hartman, 1997) are

DOI: 10.4324/9781003404842-3

well-suited for accommodating the role of context and vulnerability in the study of human developmental processes that undergird identity development.

Bronfenbrenner's EST identifies a series of nested, interacting contexts in which individuals exist and develop over time. With the individual at the center, his conceptualization of varied systems—the macrosystem, exosystem, mesosystem, and microsystem—exists within the chronosystem, considered the outermost ring constituting the societal events and phenomena that occur over history. Within this approach, shocks would occur in the chronosystem, impacting developmental trajectories.

Through the lens of EST, the Great Recession and COVID-19 constitute shocks in the chronosystem reverberating through other nested systems that frame young adults' developmental contexts. The other nested systems are populated with entities that are accessed as young adults pursue postsecondary pathways (schools, parks, stores, hospitals, etc.) at the formative stages of life and career planning. Figure 3.1 illustrates the cross-cutting effect of the Great Recession and COVID-19 on the nested systems articulated by EST.

Bronfenbrenner credits Vygotsky, who emphasized the "sociohistorical evolution of the mind" (Vygotsky & Cole, 1978) as critical to understanding of the microsystem in development. Bronfenbrenner states that the "potential options for

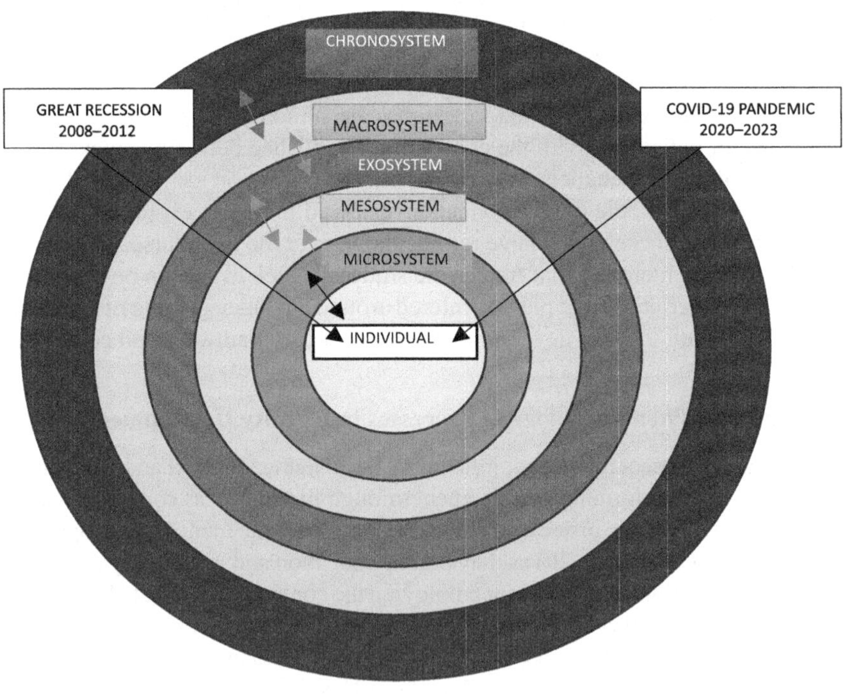

Figure 3.1 EST and Shock Events

individual development are defined and delimited by the possibilities available in a given culture at a given point in its history" (Bronfenbrenner, 1993, p. 25). Hence, EST accommodates consideration of events that occur in the chronosystem and the role of time in the shaping the developmental trajectories of individuals. (There will be further discussion of this concept when addressing the contribution of Glen Elder's life course research.)

Spencer's PVEST holds as basic tenets that all humans are vulnerable. Phenomenology is a core aspect of the theory that indicates individual-specific determined meaning making of experiences with phenomena in lived contexts. PVEST further holds that the presence or absence of supports directly impacts how individuals make meaning of risks, influencing their ability to adapt to changes and cope with risks as they develop identities and address developmental tasks as they advance through the life course. PVEST provides particularly relevant insights as an identity-focused cultural ecological theoretical perspective (ICE). Given diverse contexts and development-specific meaning making among diverse populations, PVEST affords a lens for the cultural framing and nuanced interpretations made of individuals' developmental status-specific processes. It allows for the interpretive unfolding of meanings made of contextual and developmental experiences as each individual progresses across the life course while addressing shared human development tasks. Significantly, the latter may be either impeded by risks and challenges or scaffolded by privilege as a function of group membership (see Spencer, 1995, 1999, 2006, 2008, Spencer et al., 2006; Spencer, Dupree, & Hartmann, 1997). Figure 3.2 shows Phenomenological Variant of Ecological Systems Theory.

As suggested, Spencer's PVEST underscores the criticality of considering the subjective efforts at making meaning of life's events, particularly during a period of accelerated exposure to novel tasks and risks requiring effective social cognition skills. The cultivation of coping processes for encountering challenges and risks informs the importance of Spencer's ICE perspective, which acknowledges the critical simultaneity of the interplay and linkage among "culture, context and normative psychosocial developmental processes" (Spencer, 1999, p. 43). Indeed, Spencer et al., in noting the integration of a phenomenological perspective with Bronfenbrenner's EST, notes "the synthesis . . . helps to acknowledge the critical and undergirding role of developmental changes in social cognition, multi-level social context character and content, and stage-relevant social experiences that differentially influence meaning making processes across the life course" (Spencer et al., 1997, p. 818; also, Spencer, 1995, 2006, 2008, Spencer et al., 2006). Additionally, Spencer acknowledges the importance of the cultural context, particularly for youth of color who encounter exacerbated risks "dissonance-producing environments" (Spencer, 1999, p. 44). A key question for this book, then, is how events of the Great Recession and COVID-19 exacerbated the particular risks and challenges encountered in developmental contexts during young

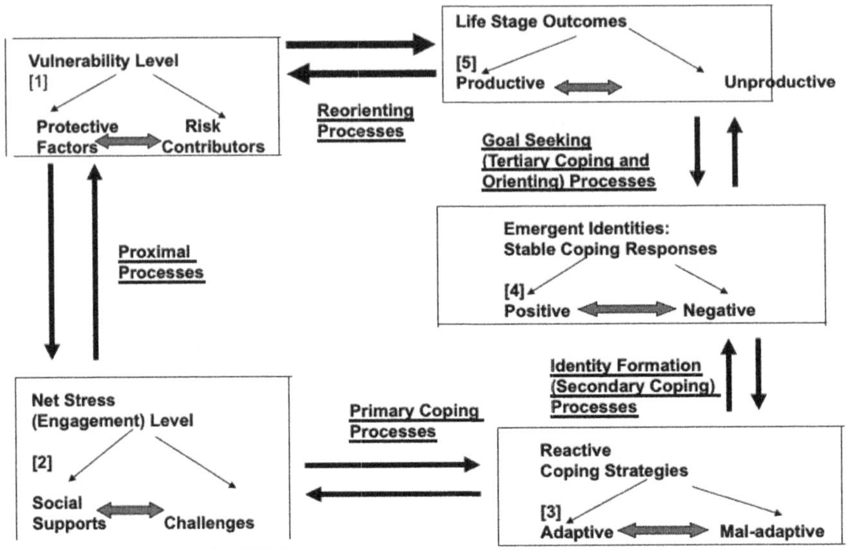

Figure 3.2 Processes Emphasizing: Phenomenological Variant of Ecological Systems Theory (PVEST)

Source: Spencer & Harpalani, 2004; Spencer, 2006

adulthood, which could lead to adaptive (e.g., staying enrolled in postsecondary education) or maladaptive (e.g., dropping out of school and not pursuing work or other endeavor) coping. There is also the question of how shocks can render binary constructs of adaptive/maladaptive unproductive for ascertaining the effect of shocks. For example, a student who returns home to care for a family member and suspends attending classes displays what could be considered a highly adaptive choice from a family bond connection, but maladaptive in terms of the developmental and material benefits that accrue from advanced education. That is to say, an action taken can be both adaptive and maladaptive at the same time depending on the nature of risk being engaged where, in this case, the seemingly maladaptive choice to stop out of school can reveal highly adaptive processes at work. As such, ascertaining the nature and character of risk along with meaning making that occurs is of critical importance, especially understanding that no individual possesses absolute knowledge in the moment. For this reason, PVEST serves as the motivating theoretical framework for opening up discernment of these meaning making processes. Further, PVEST's acknowledgement of Erikson's Theory of Psychosocial Development is aided in this book by Havighurst's insights on the developmental tasks undertaken to achieve adult status, speaking to the criticality of the setting and achievement of milestones and overcoming obstacles as part of the developmental work undertaken by youths (Havighurst, 1953). Masten's discussion of resilience provides an interesting perspective on the process of building resilience, which tends to have a positive connotation, when in fact, she asserts, there can be a "price of adversity" at work (Masten, 2014).

While Bronfenbrenner, Spencer, and Masten highlight context, vulnerability, and resilience that frame this study of the effects of a psychohistoric shock on identity development, it is useful to consider the specific dimensions that characterize sociocultural context and the implications of instability and inequality that a shock can cause. Indeed, the sociocultural context is inextricably linked to social, political, and economic events of the Great Recession and COVID-19. P.M. Greenfield's research examines the implications of sociocultural change, identifying two major contexts "one in which families stay put while the sociocultural environment changes and one in which families immigrate to a different sociocultural environment" (Greenfield, 2009) that were necessarily impacted by the economic events of 2008. A key question, then, is how consideration of context shifts how to investigate emerging adult identities.

Bronfenbrenner highlights Glen Elder's *Children of the Great Depression* as an exemplar of research that utilized a "person-process-context" approach to understand the human developmental effects of an early 20th Century shock, the Great Depression. Elder, however, acknowledged underspecfied aspects of the life course perspective that his research advanced. In his reflections on the concept in the chapter "Beyond 'Children of the Great Depression'," Elder acknowledges that early manifestations of the life course theory that emerged from *Children of the Great Depression* did not consider the complexity of the sequencing of life stages:

> Each person generally occupies multiple roles at the same time, whether spouse and parent or spouse and employee. These concurrent roles are not part of the life cycle concept. Consequently, it did not orient research to the management of multiple roles (Elder, 1999, p. 314).

Economic Distress and Families

The edited volume, *Children of the Great Recession* (Garfinkle, McLanahan, & Wimer, 2016), Conger and Conger's longitudinal study of families in rural Iowa (Conger & Conger, 2002), and Elder and Caspi's examination of familial relationships during periods of economic stress (Elder & Caspi, 1988) explore the effect of economic distress on family dynamics and implications for children's development. The *Children of the Great Recession* tackles how families with children coped in the aftermath of the economic shock. Utilizing data from the Fragile Families and Child Well-Being dataset, this edited volume centers around the application of the family stress model to understand the experiences of families with children at ages one, three, five, and nine. The Conger and Conger study examined how parents coped with economically induced distress had direct implications for their families' level of resilience and stability during times of hardship in rural Iowa. While the study identified the critical role of parenting to support a positive transition to adulthood for their children, the research focused primarily on familial relationships and dynamics, and did not provide insights on the implications of these relationships on the children's education planning after high school. Additionally, the sample in the Conger and Conger study was exclusively European American (White), and as such, the generalizability of the findings to other demographic groups is limited. Elder and Caspi continue Elder's examination of the effects of economic stress on families during the Great Depression in their article presenting a framework for studying the linkages among economic stress, social change, and individual development. The analytic framework proposed by the authors acknowledges the importance of including precursor events and contexts (i.e., the macrosocial) that increase risk and create "deprivational effects" as families are able or unable to adapt to less income. These financial shocks create stress within familial relationships that inform how family members, collectively, shape developmental trajectories for children (i.e., microsocial), either minimizing or exacerbating risk introduced by an adverse economic event. Elder and Caspi acknowledge that the generalizability of the study findings is limited by a sample comprised solely of White respondents. The social climate in the U.S. also changed dramatically between the Great Depression and the Great Recession, with landmark court decisions and legislation in education, voting rights, and civil rights allowing for greater and fuller participation by members of the diverse population in U.S. society.

Across these works, the authors draw attention to the childhood and adolescent periods, emphasizing how family coping mechanisms framed the developmental trajectories for the youth under study, but they do not focus on transitions after high school. How young adults who experience economic distress events at the point when they are transitioning to postsecondary education is a gap that Cozzolino, Smith, and Crosnoe (2018) sought to fill in their study of the Great Recession's impact by examining the college enrollment and persistence rates among 18- to 21-year-olds. Cozzolino et al. (2018) are more broadly interested in the implications of the Great Recession on the intergenerational transmission of inequality. The authors utilize a national, longitudinal dataset, the National Longitudinal Survey of Youth 1979—Young Adult cohort, to ascertain the relationship between family stability and the odds of young adults enrolling and persisting in college. The authors observe higher odds of enrollment, but these findings vary geographically and by the family's level of resilience, demonstrating that family stability makes a difference. Their study does not explore how individual young adults made meaning of the role of education and work for planning their future pursuits after high school. It also presupposes the pursuit of postsecondary education as a normative path while for many young adults, as cited in the Census data discussed in the introduction, going to college is not the primary path desired or pursued. For many young adults, going to work serves as the natural next step after high school.

Across these literatures, there is a revisiting and revising of the nature of adolescent and young adult development. These theories set forth that individual identity development occurs across a broad constellation of settings and conditions that constitute the nested contexts (e.g., home, school, and work) that individuals navigate as they engage in attainment of their milestones. This attainment process and the associated person-context dynamics of postsecondary education attainment in particularly are re-oriented during shocks are of primary interest here.

Among those works that specifically focused on economic shocks and human development processes, none delve deeply into young adult identity development that accompanies the pursuit of education and work trajectories after high school for diverse young adults. As such, there is no way to understand how those experiences frame how the young adults mitigate the risk introduced, or exacerbated, by shocks.

Human Development, Identity Development, and Context

This book focuses on the postsecondary pathways of 18- to 20-year-olds after high school graduation during two shock periods, the Great Recession and the COVID-19 pandemic, which occurred eleven years after the Great Recession was declared over.

The first two research questions (How were the post-secondary education and working patterns for low-income, high-achieving young adults shaped by the Great Recession in comparison to their high-income counterparts?; How did the Great Recession impact education planning for young adults between the ages of 18 and 20, the key age range for college going?) leverage the unique data available in the PSID Transition to Adulthood (TA) supplement, regarding the impact of the Great Recession on education planning. Because the dataset contains information on patterns of education and employment pursuits among 18- to 20-year-old young adults, it is possible to situate these patterns in the context of how the young adults did, or did not, alter their education plans because of the Great Recession. The study explores how those choices evolved during and after the Great Recession by analyzing data from the 2005, 2007, 2009, 2011, and 2013 cohorts in the PSID TA supplement. The data are bounded by an eight-year period and examine the response data captured at the time of each survey round. It is important to note that the study does not presuppose that all young adults are homogenous in their prior experiences or contexts which frame and influence their young adulthood transition.

The findings of the quantitative component frame the design of the qualitative component, which addresses the research question "Eleven years after the Great

Recession ended, have there been any changes in the factors that inform education planning for young adults between the ages of 18 and 20?". Through data captured in semi-structured interviews, this component included young adults from multiple racial and ethnic minority groups, as well as diverse immigration statuses (where reported) to ensure the inclusion of diverse perspectives on young adulthood as understood and experienced by young adults during the COVID-19 global pandemic. The findings of the quantitative component inform the content of the protocol deployed in the qualitative component of this study and the subsequent summary of results.

The research questions in this book are focused on understanding identity development in context, particularly temporal context, i.e., how does a shock event frame diverse, young adults' understanding of their required developmental tasks as young adults? Building upon insights from interviews with diverse young adults at the time of the shock, it is possible to advance a novel theory of identity development that is anchored in data captured from participants as they framed their identities while juggling multiple roles, as students, family members, and workers, while discerning their education paths and career goals. It is the data on their challenges, risks, and supports, which serve as protective factors that reveal insights on the coping strategies critical for stable identity development under dynamic conditions.

References

American Academy of Pediatrics Council on Child and Adolescent Health. (1988). American Academy of Pediatrics Council on Child and Adolescent Health: Age limits of pediatrics. *Pediatrics*, *81*(5), 736.

American Psychological Association. (2002). Developing adolescents: A reference for professionals, *47*. https://doi.org.proxy.uchicago.edu/10.1037/e327792004-001.

Bronfenbrenner, U. (1986). Ecology of the family as a context for human development. *Research Perspectives. Developmental Psychology*, *22*(6), 723–742. https://doi.org.proxy.uchicago.edu/10.1037/0012–1649.22.6.723.

Bronfenbrenner, U. (1993). The ecology of cognitive development: Research models and fugitive findings. In R. H. Wozniak & K. W. Fischer (Eds.), *Development in context: Acting and thinking in specific environments*. London: Lawrence Erlbaum Associates, Inc.

Conger, R. D., & Conger, K. J. (2002). Resilience in midwestern families: Selected findings from the first decade of a prospective, longitudinal study. *Journal of Marriage and Family*, *64*, 361–373. https://doi.org/10.1111/j.1741-3737.2002.00361.x.

Cozzolino, E., Smith, C., & Crosnoe, R. (2018). Family related disparities in college enrollment across the great recession. *Sociological Perspectives*, *61*(5), 689–710.

Elder, G. H. J., Bronfenbrenner, U., & Clausen, J. A. (1999). *Children of the great depression: Social change in life experience* (25th Anniversary ed.). Boulder, CO: Westview Press.

Elder, G. H., & Caspi, A. (1988). Economic stress in lives: Developmental perspectives. *Journal of Social Issues*, *44*(4), 25–45. https://doi.org.proxy.uchicago.edu/10.1111/j.1540-4560.1988.tb02090.x.

Erikson, E. H. (1950). *Childhood in society*. New York: Norton.

Erikson, E. H. (1968). *Identity: Youth and crisis*. New York: Norton and Company.

Garfinkel, I., McLanahan, S., & Wimer, C. (2016). *Children of the great recession*. Chicago: Russell Sage Foundation.

Greenfield, P. M. (2009). Linking social change and developmental change: Shifting pathways of human development. *Developmental Psychology*, *45*(2), 401–418.

Havighurst, R. J. (1953). *Human development and education*. New York: McKay.

Masten, A. S. (2014). Global perspectives on resilience in children and youth. *Child Development, 85*(1), 6–20.

Spencer, M. B. (1995). Old issues and new theorizing about African American youth: A phenomenological variant of ecological systems theory. In R. L. Taylor (Ed.), *African—American youth: Their social and economic status in the United States*. Westport, CT: Praeger.

Spencer, M. B. (1999). Social and cultural influences on school adjustment: The application of an identity-focused cultural ecological perspective. *Educational Psychologist*, *1*, 43.

Spencer, M. B. (2006). Phenomenology and ecological systems theory: Development of diverse groups. In R. M. Lerner & W. Damon (Eds.), *Handbook of child psychology, vol. 1: Theoretical models of human development*, 6th ed. (pp. 829–893). New York: Wiley Publishers.

Spencer, M. B. (2008). Phenomenology and ecological systems theory: Development of diverse groups. In W. Damon & R. M. Lerner (Eds.), *Child and adolescent development: An advanced course* (pp. 696–735). New York: Wiley Publishers.

Spencer, M. B., Dupree, D., & Hartmann, T. (1997). A Phenomenological Variant of Ecological Systems Theory (PVEST): A self-organization perspective in context. *Development and Psychopathology*, *4*, 817.

Spencer, M. B., Harpalani, V., Cassidy, E., Jacobs, C., Donde, S., Goss, T. N., Muñoz-Miller, M. M., Charles, N., & Wilson, S. (2006). Understanding vulnerability and resilience from a normative development perspective: Implications for racially and ethnically diverse youth. In D. Cicchetti & D. J. Cohen (Eds.), *Handbook of developmental psychopathology, vol. 1: Theory and method*, 2nd ed. (pp. 627–672). Hoboken, NJ: Wiley Publishers.

Vygotsky, L. S., & Cole, M. (1978). *Mind in society: The development of higher psychological processes*. Cambridge, MA: Harvard University Press.

4 Study Design and Implementation

Methods

The purpose of this mixed-methods study is to ascertain the identity development implications of shocks on postsecondary education pursuits. By situating postsecondary education in the context of the young adulthood developmental period, this research discerns if 18- to 20-year-olds make changes to their education plans in response to an exogenous shock, i.e., the Great Recession and COVID-19, and, if so, why and how adjustments were made to postsecondary education plans. The investigation involves analyzing survey data and conducting a series of semi-structured interviews to determine the durability of findings across shock events. The quantitative data findings frame the design of the qualitative component as an explanatory, phenomenological study utilizing a purposive sample of diverse young adults between the ages of 18- and 20-year-olds to understand their postsecondary education planning adaptations in the wake of the dual exogenous shocks of a recession and global pandemic in 2021. Specifically, the qualitative component serves to expand the categories of responses that can be derived from participants based on their own framing of the young adulthood period.

This research study applies an adapted version of Explanatory Sequential Design (Creswell & Creswell, 2018), a two-phased mixed-methods design that relies upon the findings from the quantitative to frame the qualitative component data collection and analysis in order to provide a more complete understanding of the phenomena under study. The approach calls for the utilization of the same sample to inform the key components of the quantitative and qualitative phases and following the sequenced steps of:

1) Quantitative data collection and analysis
2) Identify results for follow-up
3) Qualitative data collection and analysis
4) Interpret results—How qualitative explains quantitative

DOI: 10.4324/9781003404842-4

This study carried out an Adapted Explanatory Sequential Design because two different participant groups are studied, as opposed to utilizing the same sample for the qualitative and quantitative components. It is also important to note that the qualitative design is structured not to correct the quantitative component or re-set it but rather to delve into aspects of the research questions were under-interrogated by the quantitative findings. In the case of this research, the quantitative analysis (i.e., lack of accessibility to "Other" responses that contain nuanced insights beyond the closed response categories on how respondents adapted their education plans because of the Great Recession) precedes the qualitative phase (i.e., ability to probe how participants make meaning of exogenous shocks in their developmental contexts). As such, the two components are not brought into direct comparison, rather they are examined to derive unique insights that each phase is uniquely positioned to examine. In sum, while these distinctions across modes exist in the Adapted Explanatory Sequential Design, each study phase examines how young adults encounter novel risks and challenges resulting from exogenous shocks that occur in their developmental contexts, influencing their achievement of the postsecondary education milestones and how they make meaning of their progression to their goals.

Mixed Methods: A Brief Overview of the Approach

Mixed methods has its roots in varied disciplines in the social sciences (Creswell & Creswell, 2018; Small, 2011; Teddlie & Tashakkori, 2009). Indeed, the utilization of mixed methods engages the strengths and limitations of the quantitative and qualitative methods (Yoshikawa, Weisner, Kalil, & Way, 2008). The adoption of a mixed-methods approach lends itself to the research questions posed in this book, particularly related to the attributes of qualitative research to investigate the identity development processes underway during the transition to adulthood. Indeed, Kroger and Marcia (2011) highlight the power of qualitative research to support probing necessary for theoretically motivated research on identity development, facilitating further investigation into constructs of import in service to the theoretical question, instead of the method being the end unto itself. Arnett, citing Hammack, notes the methodological advantages of including a qualitative component in the study of the transition to adulthood when observing that "the narrative approach is a perfect methodological fit for the topic of identity development because it enables researchers to investigate identity development in the depth the topic requires" (Hammack, 2008, as cited in Arnett, 2015, p. 62). Arnett continues:

> By allowing people to tell their stories, researchers are able to discern how people perceive the parts of themselves—in love, work, and ideology—fit together into a coherent self. The narrative approach has the potential to fulfill

> Erikson's original vision of identity development as taking place through adolescents and emerging adults reflecting on the important people they have identified with throughout childhood, evaluating their abilities and interests, and seeking to find a match between.
>
> (Arnett, 2015, p. 63).

In the qualitative component, thematic analysis highlights participants' responses to questions about their experiences and perception of risks as well as access to supports during a period of exogenous shock. Together with the quantitative findings, the results of this mixed-method study provides insights on possible alterations made to education pathways, and the implications for identity development, because of exogenous shocks that collided with diverse young adults' transition to adulthood.

Following this overview of mixed methods and the rationale for utilizing this approach, this chapter then provides a description of the quantitative data and analytic approach, followed by a summary of the qualitative procedures. The findings of this mixed methods study, presented in Chapter 5, provide insights on alterations to the young adulthood developmental period for diverse young adults during periods of exogenous shocks.

Quantitative Component

As noted in Chapter 4, the quantitative component addresses the following two research questions:

- How were the post-secondary education and working patterns for low-income, high-achieving young adults shaped by the Great Recession in comparison to their high-income counterparts?
- How did the Great Recession impact education planning for young adults between the ages of 18 and 20, the key age range for college going?

This is accomplished by analyzing the PSID TA dataset for the 2005, 2007, 2009, 2011, and 2013 rounds of data collection (Panel Survey of Income Dynamics, 2021). Specifically, the study examines responses to questions about postsecondary education and postsecondary work for 18- to 20-year-olds before and after the Great Recession. The 2005 and 2007 data provide insight on the pre-recession education and work patterns of respondents. In the 2009 survey round, the TA supplement began capturing information on the impact of the Great Recession. Specifically, the survey asked respondents the following question:

> Has the current recession changed your educational plans? If Yes, How?
>
> - Dropped out of school
> - Returned to or enrolled in school
> - Postponed school

- Stayed in school
- Changed major
- Borrowed money
- Other

The responses to this item for the 2011 and 2013 waves provide a post-recessionary picture of the postsecondary education and work patterns of the respondents. Altogether, these five survey rounds enhance the study of trends before, during, and after the Great Recession. Of particular interest is how enrolled young adults report how they made changes to their education plans, including not pursuing further education, because of the Great Recession. As noted earlier, it is understood that pathways are not always linear and context plays a role; however, this study restricts its focus to just understanding how respondents altered their education plans.

As an analytic category, "high achieving young adult" is defined as an 18- to 20-year-old enrolled in college. The working, 18- to 20-year-old group is comprised of young adults who report working but are not enrolled in college. To define the low- and high-income groups for 18- to 20-year-olds, this book utilizes the U.S. Census' calculation of median family income for each PSID survey year included in the analysis. The PSID provides total family income for the year immediately prior to the survey year (e.g., 2005 annual income variable captures income reported for 2004). As such, the Census median income data to be used in this analysis is associated with the PSID reported income year, not the survey year. Table 4.1 provides a summary of the U.S. median income utilized in this book project.

It is understood that income is not the sole indicator of the resources present and understood as such in an individual's context and is therefore not synonymous with socioeconomic status (SES). Indeed, research on SES has highlighted the importance of developing SES measures that factor in various dimensions of the construct (e.g., APA, 2007; NCES, 2012). Rather than a singular variable, SES can be considered a composite of three primary elements—family income, parental occupation, and parental education (NCES, 2012). Indeed, other categories of

Table 4.1 Census Median Income by PSID Survey Year

PSID Survey Year	*PSID Reported Income Year*	*Census Median for PSID Reported Income Year*
2005	2004	$44,389
2007	2006	$48,451
2009	2008	$51,726
2011	2010	$51,114
2013	2012	$51,371

Source: PSID TA Supplement, 2017; U.S. Census, 2015

Table 4.2 Summary Statistics for Income

PSID Survey Year	*N*	*Mean*	*Std. Dev*	*Min*	*Max*
2005					
Above Median	415	$111,231	$100,743	$44,500	$1,247,797
Below Median	317	$23,098	$11,761	$0	$44,282
2007					
Above Median	375	$131,624	$177,063	$48,500	$2,133,500
Below Median	320	$23,893	$13,093	$0	$48,400
2009					
Above Median	376	$125,701	$114,707	$52,115	$1,324,200
Below Median	298	$26,899	$14,009	$0	$51,500
2011					
Above Median	347	$123,125	$84,403	$51,400	$1,460,000
Below Median	336	$25,040	$14,488	$0	$51,076
2013					
Above Median	332	$128,166	$182,000	$51,850	$3,222,000
Below Median	262	$25,864	$14,722	$0 *	$50,700

Source: PSID TA Supplement, 2017. Note: The amount of "−$11,500" appearing in the dataset is coded as "$0" for this table. The negative figure for income may be owed to an errant data entry not addressed in standard data cleaning protocols

resources—such as neighborhood SES and subjective understanding of SES—extend the conceptualization of not just how SES is measured, but how it is understood and experienced. Building on the geographic features of SES, the Opportunity Atlas further broadens how to understand SES by factoring in economic mobility in various geographic contexts over time (Chetty, Friedman, Hendren, Jones, & Porter, 2018). Indeed, there is now a need to include not just geographic variablilty, but to also account for the presence or absence of the digital divide, along with access to clean water, air, and green spaces, as additional indicators of essential resources. While various measures and conceptualizations of SES exist, for the purposes of this study component, income served as an indicator of financial resources obtained primarily through working.

The procedure carried out in the analysis entailed first summarizing the descriptive statistics of the enrolled TA sample. The next step in the analysis entailed conducting chi-square analyses to ascertain statistically significant differences ($p < 0.05$) by two broad income categories: above median income and below median income for the 2009, 2011, and 2013 data collection rounds to ascertain how enrollment patterns varied by income level.

Qualitative Component

The qualitative component was comprised of five primary activities—respondent recruitment, data collection and processing, coding, including validity and reliability checks, data analysis reporting. A total of 18 respondents from across the U.S. who either attended two-year community colleges or four-year baccalaureate-granting institutions completed interviews. Employing an Adaptive Explanatory Design (described earlier), the interview protocol applied a phenomenological strategy (Creswell, 2009) to investigate the lived experiences of study participants as they structured their experiences and consciousness of same, thus making decisions regarding their postsecondary experiences.

The original study plan called for the identification of two to three urban areas for study subject recruitment. At the time participant recruitment was to commence, the COVID-19 global pandemic halted travel and in-person, site-based recruitment and interviewing was no longer possible due to public health emergency closures nationwide. The study staff undertook a study redesign to adapt the data collection plan to a remote data collection strategy that allowed for data collection to proceed in keeping with public health guidelines while maintaining the integrity of the study design objectives in adherence with the research questions. The redesign shifted the interview mode from in-person to a secure, virtual meeting platform. Recruitment activities occurred through email and over the phone. Coding and analysis took place in a web-based collaborative workspace with access restricted to study staff only.

Participant Eligibility and Interview Administration Arrangements

The study relied upon an inclusive standard for respondent participation and welcomed diverse participants. Persons were eligible to participate regardless of sex, gender identity, disability status, race, ethnicity, immigration status, or national origin. At the time of scheduling an interview, the study solicited accommodation information from eligible participants to ensure that the online meeting arrangements were responsive to participant needs and requirements. Additionally, the study staff encouraged participants to identify a location for the interview that met their privacy needs. Participants received a $30 gift card in appreciation for their participation and cooperation with making any necessary arrangements to participate virtually. While the consent form notified respondents that the gift card would be distributed even if the respondent suspended the interview prior to answering all questions, all study participants who started an interview responded to all items in the protocol.

After obtaining Institutional Review Board (IRB) approval to ensure that the study conformed with human subjects protections, study staff shared study recruitment material with two postsecondary institutional personnel (midsize and large urban areas), programs that support college access and persistence among first-generation students (midsize and large urban area) and organizations that serve at-risk youth (large urban area). Study staff coordinated with site-based research personnel to obtain institution-specific IRB approval prior to advancing with direct outreach to students. After gaining approval to proceed, study staff disseminated notices about the study to relevant staff and posted study information on available email lists and listservs, including those that serve student affinity groups (e.g., African American Student Associations, Latinx Student Association, First-Generation Student Associations) to ensure that notice of the study was shared broadly among diverse student communities. Staff also reached out to two organizations that served 18- to 20-year-old persons who were working or seeking job retraining, but not enrolled in a degree-granting program. These efforts to recruit non-enrolled young adults were not successful. The main outreach document, "PESGR Study Announcement and FAQ," provided an overview of the study and key information (see Appendix). All outreach notices provided a study-specific email address for study inquiries and to schedule interview appointments. Throughout all recruitment steps, potential respondents were notified of the voluntary nature of their participation and the confidentiality of their responses.

Risk Minimization and Respondent Protection in Virtual Interview Context

The study design lent itself to adapting to COVID-19 restrictions on travel and in-person engagement, facilitated by the availability of virtual conferencing tools. Respondents established a date and time for their interview that was convenient to them. All participant requests for re-scheduling interviews were honored by study research staff. Staff were flexible in making alternate arrangements if persons had schedule changes that necessitated identifying a new interview appointment. This was a rare occurrence, but it was always accommodated.

In terms of sensitive items, the protocol only asked questions related to respondents' attitudes and opinions about school, work, and life goals, and the interviews did not pose any sensitive questions related to private, personal activities.

Additionally, interviews were one-on-one, and not in a group setting, so no persons outside of the interviewer and the participant were included in the interview meeting. Procedures to mitigate risk included empowering respondents to not respond to questions without penalty, i.e., they would still be entitled to the incentive should they suspend the interview at any point, and encouraging respondents to identify a location for the interview that suited their privacy needs. Also, hotline numbers were provided should further assistance be sought by respondents.

Respondent Recruitment

The study design called for the selection of a purposive sample of 20 study participants between the ages of 18 and 20 years old at the time of screener administration. A total of 23 individuals sent participation inquiries to the study email account. Two individuals were ineligible to participate due to age, two persons completed screening but did not schedule an interview appointment, and one person screened into the study and scheduled an appointment but did not appear for the interview. The remaining 18 persons confirmed eligibility to participate and completed an interview.

Study staff coordinated with eligible persons to identify an interview appointment window that best fit with participants' schedules. All interviews were recorded for the purposes of data coding and analysis.

Linkage to Quantitative Component

The content of the semi-structured interview protocol was shaped by the results of the quantitative study, which are reviewed in the next chapter. Of particular interest was ascertaining the undefined components of the diverse, young adults' phenomenological processing in response to the question of how they changed their education plans in response to the Great Recession. The PSID descriptive analysis results revealed that "Other" was the highest frequency response to the question in 2013 indicating that there were other adjustments being made that were not captured by the response categories offered. As such, the questions posed to participants about the effects of the global pandemic and linked recession on education plans were intentionally set as open-ended items. This approach avoided any possible satisficing on the part of participants whose responses might be guided or influenced by closed response categories. As a result, the qualitative component centered respondents' insights on the phenomena under study, and, as a result, it is participants' own answers to these questions that frame the thematic categories that are derived from the qualitative interviews.

Participant Recruitment Materials and Strategies

The study utilized a set of recruitment materials to ensure participants were fully informed about what was entailed in study participation. The PESGR Study Announcement and Frequently Asked Questions flyer (Appendix) provided an overview of the study's purpose, eligibility criteria, voluntary nature of participation, honorarium, interview length, and further information on participation. The flyer also contained a list of resources that participants could contact for additional supports if needed. The list of supports included the USDA National Hunger Hotline, the National Hotline for Mental Health Support and/or Substance Use Disorders, the National Suicide Prevention Hotline, and a hotline number to obtain a referral to a housing counseling agency in a participant's area.

Each participant that screened into the study as eligible received a consent form (Appendix). The consent form provided a study description and participation requirements, underscoring the voluntary nature of participation, along with information on human subjects protection provisions in place to assure respondent confidentiality. The form also asked that respondents provide a response to whether they consented to have their recording used in the reports and if they agreed to being contacted in the future for follow ups.

Interview Protocol

The interview protocol for the study can be found in the Appendix. Its content was organized into four sections:

Screener and Introductory Section
Demographic and Background Information
Education and Work Plans
Resource Level and Supports

The interview captured information on the risks and challenges students identified relative to the pursuit of their education and work goals. The timing of the data collection period coincided with the linked exogenous shocks: the COVID-19 pandemic and the ensuing economic recession.

The instrument opened with a screener to confirm the eligibility of individuals to participate in the study. In order to participate, respondents needed to be between 18 and 20 years of age. This portion of the interview provided an overview of the study's purpose, the estimated length of the interview appointment, and reminded respondents of the voluntary nature of participation. The introductory section also recorded study consent to participate in the interview and to record the interview.

The protocol asked demographic questions, including education enrollment and work statuses and their residential, education, and work location zip codes; information on how the current recession and COVID-19 global pandemic changed education and work plans; key risks and challenges to education and work goals; and perception and accessibility of key resources and supports. The theoretically motivated instrument operationalizes PVEST by focusing on capturing data on how participants make meaning of the risks they encounter, if any, as a result of the pandemic and a recession in their developmental contexts. Their responses to the exacerbated risks that emerged in their environments allows for documenting the meaning making underway, i.e., phenomenological processes, as they made sense of their next steps for their education and work. The interview allowed participants to share insights on the supports that they engaged as they navigated and coped with challenges they were encountering. There were no suspended interviews or refusals to respond to any questions.

Data Security and Processing

All recordings along with resulting raw and coded data files were stored at a secure, password-protected account that resided behind a firewall. Only team members had access to the account, and restrictions were placed on the files to allow authorized access only. All respondent materials that were coded were de-identified, with names removed from transcripts utilized for coding. Additionally, staff separated location information, i.e., zip codes, from the transcript file that would be utilized in the asset analysis component of the study.

At the time of the interview confirmation, a randomly generated identification number was assigned to each case to ensure that no respondent's personal identifying information (i.e., name, email address) was linked to individual data and coding files.

Data Coding, Validity, and Reliability

The validity and reliability of the data are critical to ensuring that study findings are interpreted to achieve accuracy and interrater reliability. All interview coding implemented an iterative process of assigning codes for close-ended items and conducting thematic analysis of open-ended responses. The coding team was comprised of the study's lead researcher and two research assistants. The research assistants were in the age range of the participant sample and enrolled in postsecondary education. Each transcript underwent a quality check to ensure full alignment with the recorded interview. Once quality checks were completed, the transcripts were assigned to coders who "owned" a group of cases. The staffing arrangement was adopted to achieve consisistency in the codes applied to participants responses (Leung, 2015).

Coders carried out thematic analyses of each transcript, creating a code frame for open-ended, verbatim responses. After an initial round of coding with two transcripts to develop the initial code frame that would guide coders' efforts, each transcript underwent coding review and assignment. The study team met on a weekly basis to share coding progress, raise questions in need of clarification, and refine the code frame. The team would also reference field notes to inform coding decisions. These notes, taken contemporaneously during the interview, included detail on any items where the interviewer probed participants for clarification or meaning. To validate assigned codes, each interviewer reviewed their counterpart's code assignments for accuracy, i.e., triangulation, saturation of the code (Small, 2011), and coherence. The third check entailed coders making edits to code assignments to ensure they appropriately conveyed participant responses and conformed to the code frame. A final review of each coder's datasets assured consistency between participant responses and code assignments.

Participant Interviews

As referenced earlier, all interviews were carried out utilizing a virtual conferencing platform that was launched from a secure server. At the start of the interview appointment, each respondent provided verbal consent to participate and to have their interview recorded. Respondents provided a response to being contacted for follow up (Yes: n = 17; No: n = 1) and to having their images or recordings shared in presentations (Yes: n = 18; No: n = 0). After the interview was completed and the recording was stopped, respondents provided the interviewer with their preferred method for receiving their $30 honorarium for participation. All but one respondent requested an electronic gift card, with one participant requesting that a gift card be mailed to their physical address.

While most interviews were conducted with video and audio recording enabled (one respondent deactivated the video recording option), only the audio recordings were transcribed. The interviews took an average of 23 minutes, with the shortest interview running for 11:30 minutes and the longest interview appointment taking 39:25 minutes. Seventeen interviews were conducted in English, and one interview was conducted in English and Spanish. The audio recordings were transcribed by a third-party transcription service with multilingual capabilities for translating the interview conducted in Spanish. Upon receipt of the individual transcript files, study staff conducted a quality control check to ensure accuracy of the transcription by comparing transcripts with the audio recording for each interview.

Participant Characteristics: Demographics, Location, Enrollment Statuses, and Resource Levels

The interview opened capturing participants' demographic information. The participant group is comprised entirely of students of color. All study participants were enrolled in postsecondary education at the time of the interview, with three participants enrolled in a two-year community college, fourteen attending a four-year institution. One participant did not specify the institution type in the interview.

The following summary presents key demographic characteristics and enrollment statuses (first-generation postsecondary student; institution type; enrollment year). Note that the specific racial/ethnic categories are presented as reported by respondents, and these are arranged below according to individual alignments with broad demographic groups.

Black/African American—4
Asian/West Asian—Kurdish/Pacific Islander/Vietnamese—6
Latino/a/x /Mexican-American—7
Black and Latinx—1

Enrollment Year:

First Year—9
Second Year—6
Third year—2
No Data—1

Additional Background Information:

Immigrants to the U.S.—4
International students—2
First-generation college students—7

Sex/Gender Identity:

Female—10
Male—8

No participants had children. When offered the opportunity to provide additional information regarding their background or other biographical information they wished to share, participants volunteered their immigration status, category of enrollment as international students or non-U.S.-born students. Seven students shared their status as first-generation college students. In the course of the interviews nine participants, or half of the group, reported being employed while enrolled. Those who were working were evenly split between first- and second-year students. Additionally, the majority of those working reported having either part-time or on-demand "gig" jobs. Table 4.3 provides additional detail this group of working students.

Students who were working distinguish the qualitative participant group from the PSID young adult groups who were sorted into discrete groups based on their status either as enrolled or working. The selection criteria for the qualitative data did not screen for participants' employment status, so the qualitative data provide insights on those students who were both enrolled and working during the COVID-19 pandemic.

Resource Levels

Participants provided information on their resource levels, responding to a question that provided a detailed description of the concept to inform how they would self-categorize. The question read:

> Resources refer to sources of income, healthcare, food, housing, or other things that help you meet your material daily needs. Do you consider your life

Table 4.3 Enrolled Working Students

Enrollment Year	*Institution Type*	*Major*	*Job*	*Job Type*
2	4 Year Private	Environmental Engineering	Youth Soccer Coach	Part Time
1	4 Year Public	Business Administration/ Architecture	Online Shop Owner	Full Time
2	2 Year Public	Psychology	Captionist	On Demand
1	4 Year Private	Computer Science	Teaching Assistant	Part Time
2	4 Year Private	International Business	Office Filing	Part Time
1	2 Year Public	Psychology	Supermarket Cashier	Part Time
1	4 Year Private	Computer Science	Tutor	On Demand
1	2 Year Public	Information Technology	School Newspaper	Part Time
2	4 Year Private	Finance	Spanish tutor	Part Time

> right now as being low resourced (not getting enough to meet daily needs), medium resourced (you're getting enough to meet daily needs), or high resourced (you have more than enough to meet your daily needs).

While the quantitative component utilized income to convey SES, the qualitative component intentionally selected a resource-centered approach to allow for study participants to frame their responses in terms of their ability to meet their daily needs, as opposed to imposing income categories that may not speak to how respondents experience material supports. The majority of study participants conveyed that they were either medium- (6) or high-resourced (8), with three respondents stating they were medium-high resourced and only one respondent reporting that they were low resourced.

A Note about Digital Nativity

The qualitative study interviews were carried out exclusively online due to COVID-19 public health safety precautions and restrictions. It is important to note that all young adults in the qualitative component of the study shared the status of "digital natives," having attended elementary and secondary school in the internet age. As such, all of the participants were fluent in communicating freely and authentically through the internet-based conferencing system that was deployed. Technical issues with internet connectivity occurred (i.e., unstable connectivity) but were very rare and did not impede the overall momentum of the interviews. In fact, those few instances where a dropped connection occurred, the participants were unfazed and easily resumed the flow of the discussion upon reconnection. (In these rare occurences the online conferencing program preserved the recording, and no data were lost when internet connections dropped.)

The digital nativity of these study participants does not presuppose unfettered access to the internet for all: the digital divide exists in the U.S., whereby many communities, frequently economically low-resourced and rural communities, do not have broadband access or the access is consistently unstable, rendering unfettered access to the intellectual, social, and commercial benefits of the internet elusive (U.S. Government Accountability Office, 2022; 2023). As such, the author acknowledges that the internet access that facilitated interview participation under COVID restrictions may have been possible through institutional means or owed to a participant's residing in a location that ensured broad internet access. Increasingly, in the overall conduct of social science research studies, digital contexts and internet accessibility matter. This domain of interaction and increased research activity demands that the ethics governing human subjects research adapt and translate to online contexts, accommodating consent requirements for research participation and study activities, particularly related to the use and distribution of video and audio data. Further, the interspersion of a screen is not the same as in-person interviews, and can alter the interviewer-participant dynamic, depending on the interviewer's comfort and ease of use with the technology. As such, additional time may be needed for training on the technical aspects of interview set up (e.g., stable internet connections, checking in for respondent comfort and burden, protocols for managing interruptions, providing appropriate security and back up provisions for recorded data) so that the participant experience is both positive and yields rich, valid data. Consideration of these factors is of particular significance in the context of an adaptive explanatory mixed-methods design, where the linkages between quantitative and qualitative data are central to addressing key research questions.

Throughout the interviews, the author took contemporaneous notes capturing observations regarding the responses and to highlight points for additional probing or clarification on terms used by respondents to ensure accuracy of participant intent when coding responses. As a result, the findings presented in the next chapter center the authentic perpectives of participants. While the nature of their interview contexts varied, from bedrooms to dorm rooms, all participants showed tremendous commitment to this research and its goal to improve understanding of young adult developmental experiences.

Chapter 5 turns to a discussion of the study's findings with respect to the results derived from the quantitative and qualitative components.

References

American Psychological Association. (2007). Report of the APA task force on socioeconomic status, *46*. https://doi.org.proxy.uchicago.edu/10.1037/e582962010-001.

Arnett, J. J. (2015). Identity development from adolescence to emerging adulthood: What we know and (especially) what we don't know. In K. C. McLean & M. U. Syed (Eds.),

The Oxford handbook of identity development. New York, NY: Oxford University Press.

Chetty, R., Friedman, J. N., Hendren, N., Jones, M. R., & Porter, S. R. (2018). The opportunity atlas: Mapping the childhood roots of social mobility (No. w25147). National Bureau of Economic Research.

Creswell, J. W. (2009). *Research design: Qualitative, quantitative, and mixed methods approaches* (3rd ed.). Thousand Oaks, CA: Sage.

Creswell, J. W., & Creswell, J. D. (2018). *Research design: Qualitative, quantitative, and mixed methods approaches* (5th ed.). Thousand Oaks, CA: SAGE Publications, Inc.

Hammack, P. L. (2008). Narrative and the cultural psychology of identity. *Personality and Social Psychology Review*, *12*, 222–247.

The Institute for Social Research, University of Michigan. (2021). *Panel study of income dynamics, public use dataset*. Ann Arbor, MI: The Institute for Social Research, University of Michigan

Kroger, J., & Marcia, J. E. (2011). The identity statuses: Origins, meanings, and interpretations. *Handbook of Identity Theory and Research*, *31*. https://doi.org.proxy.uchicago.edu/10.1007/978-1-4419-7988-9_2.

Leung, L. (2015). Validity, reliability, and generalizability in qualitative research. *Journal of family medicine and primary care*, *4*(3), 324.

National Center for Education Statistics (ED). (2012). *Improving the Measurement of Socioeconomic Status for the National Assessment of Educational Progress: A Theoretical Foundation: Recommendations to the National Center for Education Statistics*. ERIC Clearinghouse.

Small, M. L. (2011). How to conduct a mixed methods study: Recent trends in a rapidly growing literature. *Annual Review of Sociology (Print)*, *37*, 57–86.

Teddlie, C., & Tashakkori, A. (2009). *Foundations of mixed methods research: Integrating quantitative and qualitative approaches in the social and behavioral sciences*. Los Angeles: SAGE.

U.S. Census Bureau. (2015). 2010–2014 American Community Survey 5-Year Estimates.

U.S. General Accountability Office. (2022). Broadband National Strategy Needed to Guide Federal Efforts to Reduce Digital Divide (GAO-22-104611). Report to Congressional Requesters.

U.S. General Accountability Office. (2023, February 1). Closing the Digital Divide for Millions of Americans without Broadband. Watchblog: Following the American Dollar. https://www.gao.gov/blog/closing-digital-divide-millions-americans-without-broadband.

Yoshikawa, H., Weisner, T. S., Kalil, A., & Way, N. (2008). Mixing qualitative and quantitative research in developmental science: Uses and methodological choices. *Developmental Psychology*, *44*(2), 344–354.

5 (Un)Stable Paths

Postsecondary Enrollment Experiences through the Great Recession and COVID-19

The previous chapters provided an overview of the societal impact of the Great Recession and the COVID-19 global pandemic in the U.S. and globally. These chapters also discussed how the study of postsecondary experiences during shock periods is informed by varied social scientific disciplinary traditions that describe the developmental, social, and economic implications of the pursuit of postsecondary education as a singular milestone of young adulthood in the U.S. As a marker of both academic and developmental readiness, a postsecondary credential can convey academic preparation, professional training, and maturity to assume the responsibilities, privileges, and obligations of adulthood. It is important to note that this academic credential does not convey the totality of psychological, cultural and social indicators of maturity. Other pursuits, such as apprenticing for a trade, undertaking study to prepare for a religious rite of passage or assuming familial financial responsibilities, are but a few examples of milestones that confer advancement toward adult status. Pathways such as these can overlap with educational pursuits at the secondary or postsecondary levels and can serve to augment the maturational aspects of young adult identity development. Here, in this work, specific focus is on the meaning making of the pursuit of postsecondary education for its unique identity developmental properties at the young adult developmental phase. When the pursuit of this milestone aligns with shock events, which disrupt the contexts in which the work toward these milestones is undertaken, the person-context dynamic merits examination given that meaning making processes at work frame identity developing activities. For this reason, this study undertook a series of phenomenological interviews to capture real-time data from selected participants on their experiences during the dual public health and economic shock event. The interview protocol utilized for the qualitative interview centered the key question advanced in PSID Transition to Adulthood module regarding the Great Recession: how did the event change diverse young adult education and work plans?

The phenomenological semi-structured interviews allowed for an in-depth exploration of the particular ways that a group of young adults from across the U.S. assessed risk and were able to maneuver through the uncharted territory of postsecondary education in a global pandemic. While the Great Recession was an unanticipated historic economic shock, with reverberations that collided with pre-existing

DOI: 10.4324/9781003404842-5

inequality and discrimination, it was not an unknown phenomenon: a compendium of research and policy interventions from prior recessions provided a knowledge framework to inform navigating through one of the worst economic crises in modern times (e.g., Weinberg, 2013; Farber, 2015; Passmore & Sherlund, 2016). With the pandemic, there was no handbook nor empirical research at a global level that mapped on to the scale of COVID-19, both for the rapidity of the spread of the virus across all populations as well as the struggle of governmental and public health entities to respond in a fashion commensurate with the threat. Along with political and ideological gamesmanship, this was a pandemic of epic proportions that exploited the vulnerabilities of humanity and their institutions alike.

It is helpful, then, to review the data findings regarding the effect of shocks on postsecondary plans. Chapter 4 provided a rationale and an overview of the mixed methods approach adopted for this study, Adapted Explanatory Design. The summary of the methods applied for the quantitative and qualitative approaches detailed the characteristics of the study samples, the analytic approach, and a summary of the study procedures. Following are the key findings of each study component, with a link to the research questions that each component addresses. In addition to the findings that provide insights for advancing understanding of the effect of the Great Recession and the COVID-19 global pandemic on the education plans for diverse 18- to 20- year-olds, they also set the stage for a deeper discussion regarding the implications of shocks on the young adulthood developmental period more broadly.

Riding the Wave: A National View of a Shock's Postsecondary Education Reverberations. It is useful to obtain a national view of 18- to 20-year-olds who were enrolled or working before, during, and after the Great Recession to assess how the shock impacted postsecondary education plan for this age group in particular. Findings drawn from the Transition to Adulthood module of the PSID (2017), a survey administered to a nationally representative sample, frame the broad enrollment trends and effects of the Great Recession on education planning for enrolled and working as well as non-enrolled respondents. (For further information on the design of the PSID, see Chapter 4.) These data address the first two research questions addressed in the quantitative component of the study:

- How were the post-secondary education and working patterns for *low-income, high-achieving young adults* ***shaped by the Great Recession*** in comparison to their *high-income* counterparts?
- How did the Great Recession ***impact education planning*** for young adults between the ages of 18 and 20, the key age range for college going?

Descriptive Findings

The following figures highlight enrollment trends observed in the PSID before, during, and after the Great Recession. These figures, notably Figure 5.1, affirm findings addressed in Chapter 1 that college enrollment increased during the Great Recession.

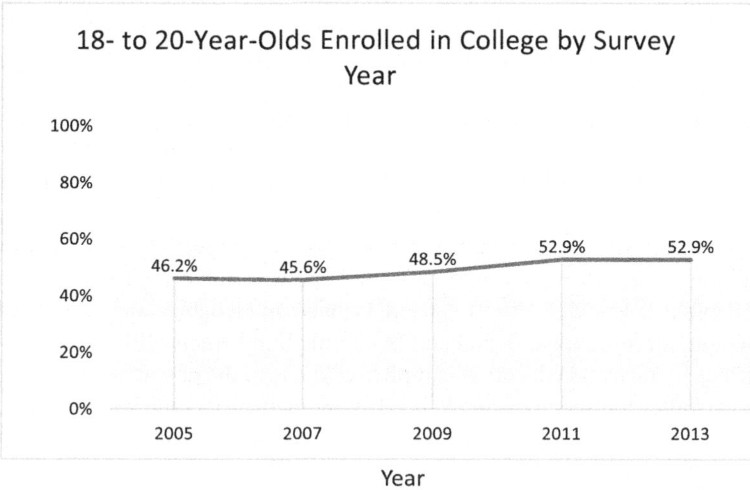

Figure 5.1 Enrollment by College Year

Source: Panel Study of Income Dynamics, public use dataset (2017). Produced and distributed by the Survey Research Center, Institute for Social Research, University of Michigan, Ann Arbor, MI.

Note: Author analysis of data

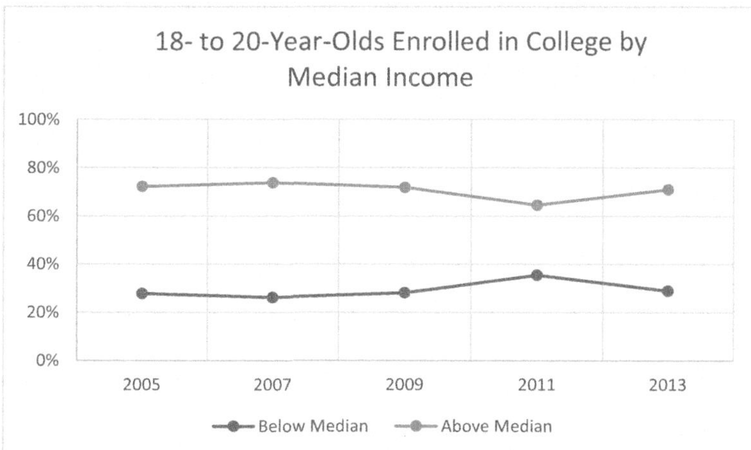

Figure 5.2 College Enrollment by Median Income

Source: Panel Study of Income Dynamics, public use dataset (2017). Produced and distributed by the Survey Research Center, Institute for Social Research, University of Michigan, Ann Arbor, MI.

Note: Author analysis of data

While Figure 5.1 shows that between 2005 and 2013, PSID 18- to 20-year-olds enrolled in college at a steadily increasing rate, with the trend plateauing by 2013, different patterns of enrollment rates emerge by income. When disaggregating by median income (Figure 5.2), a disparate pattern of enrollment appears whereby above-median-income young adults' college attendance decreases while below-median-income students' rates increase as 2011 approaches. In 2013, the rates shift between income groups as higher resourced young adults' enrollment increases as below median young adults' enrollment rates decrease. (Note: This research utilizes income as a proxy for resource levels. See Chapter 4 for a fuller discussion of the study's approach to resource level assessments.) It is possible that this indicates that the above-median-income young adults' families may have recovered income lost during the Great Recession, allowing for a return to pre-Great Recession enrollment levels for this group. Research shows that the recovery from the Great Recession was anemic and uneven, especially when comparing overall post-Great Recession household income with the prior 1990–1991 recession (Bennett & Kochhar, 2019). Indeed, Bennett and Kochhar analyses of Current Population Survey Annual Social and Economic Supplement (IPUMS) data reveal disparities by race and education completion levels in the post-recessionary period nine years after the shock event (*Ibid.*). Below-median-income young adults, who may have enrolled in college to wait out the recessionary storm, did not enroll at the same rates as the economic recovery took hold.

Changes in Education Plans among Enrolled Young Adults as a Result of the Great Recession

The PSID-TA focused on the effects of the Great Recession between 2009 and 2013. When turning attention to the central question of whether the Great Recession caused enrolled 18- to 20-year-olds to change education plans, the two income groups follow similar patterns in each survey round. Figure 5.3

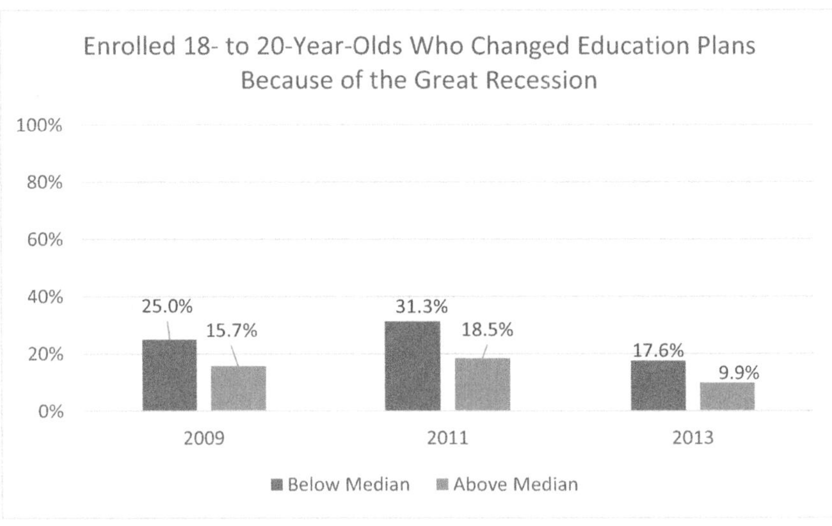

Figure 5.3 Changing Education Plans Because of the Great Recession

Source: Panel Study of Income Dynamics, public use dataset (2017). Produced and distributed by the Survey Research Center, Institute for Social Research, University of Michigan, Ann Arbor, MI.

Note: Author analysis of data

shows that in 2009, 2011, and 2013, more below-median-income students than above-median-income students reported they would change their education plans, with the highest proportions reported in 2011. Well after the recession is declared over in 2013, there is a notable drop in the proportion of young adults who report they changed their education plans, indicating perhaps that the Great Recession effect dissipated. It is not clear if this reduction is owed to the improvement in the economy or students pursuing alternate pathways, such as the military. It is consistent with the findings in Figure 5.2 showing an overall decrease in enrollment for the below-median-income group.

Across survey rounds and income categories, "Changing Major" was the most-cited option (outside of "Other, specify") reported for changing young adult's education plans (see Figures 5.4 and 5.5). For this survey item, respondents were allowed to select all that apply. In 2009 and 2011, a greater proportion of below-median-income students than above-median-income students reported that they planned to return to school, while in 2009 and 2011 proportionately less below-median-income students than above-median-income students decided to postpone school. These two findings suggest a greater interest on the part of below-median-income students to advance their education in those two rounds. However, 2013 reveals a shift: data show an increase in the proportion of below-median students who report they would postpone school compared to the proportion of above-median students who report the same. Accompanying this increase that year is a reduction in the proportion of below-median students who report they would return to schools.

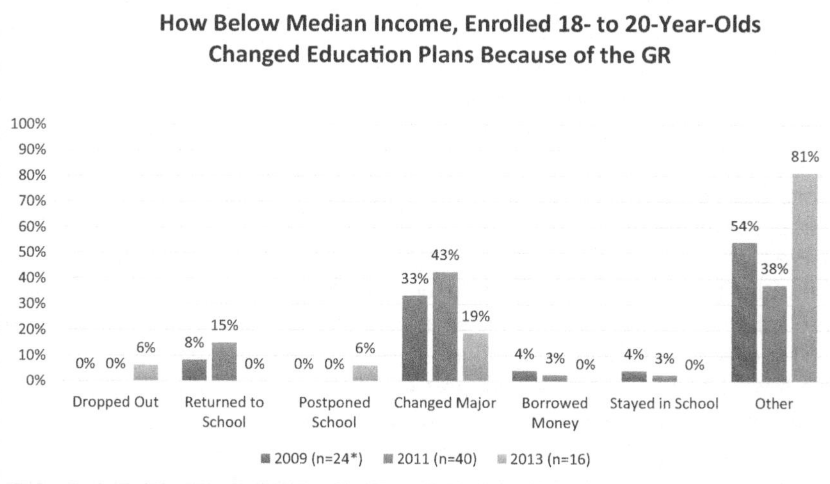

Figure 5.4 How Education Plans Changed—Below Median

Source: Panel Study of Income Dynamics, public use dataset (2017). Produced and distributed by the Survey Research Center, Institute for Social Research, University of Michigan, Ann Arbor, MI.

Note: Author analysis of data

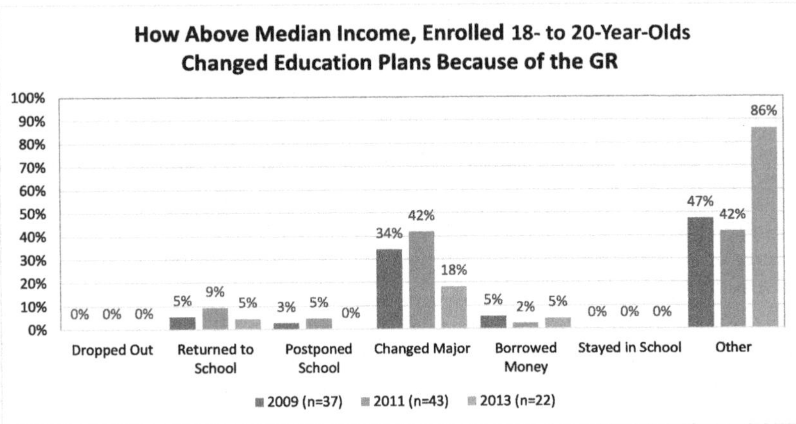

Figure 5.5 Changed Education Plans—Above Median

Source: Panel Study of Income Dynamics, public use dataset (2017). Produced and distributed by the Survey Research Center, Institute for Social Research, University of Michigan, Ann Arbor, MI.

Note: Author analysis of data

Working Young Adults and Education Planning

Those young adults in the PSID-TA sample who were not enrolled in school and were working sustained some interest in pursuing education during the period of the Great Recession. Interestingly, working young adults who reported changing their educational plans because of the Great Recession demonstrate a pattern that aligns with their enrolled counterparts: in 2009, below-median-income young adults report heightened interest in changing educational plans. For working young adults that interest tapers off as time moves further out from the onset of the Great Recession, while enrolled students' desire to change their plans peaks in 2011 before showing a decline by 2013. Figure 5.6 summarizes the proportion of working, non-enrolled young adults who were above and below median income. Before the Great Recession, young adults below median income reported working at increasing levels, with reported work activity peaking in 2011. 2013 marked a precipitous drop in this income group's work participation. It is worth noting that the actual number of respondents in this group (i.e., a total of two non-enrolled, working young adults) is small. Nonetheless, this calls attention to the need to delve further into the reason(s) for this decline in future studies.

Across the Great Recession and post-Great Recession years (2009, 2011, and 2013), most working young adults who were respondents to the TA supplement reported that the Great Recession did not cause them to change their education plans. However, when disaggregated by income categories, an interesting pattern emerges whereby a slightly larger proportion of below-median-income young adults who were working and not enrolled reported changing their education plans as a result of the Great Recession than their above-median-income counterparts. Figures 5.7 through 5.9 illustrate these findings. These suggest

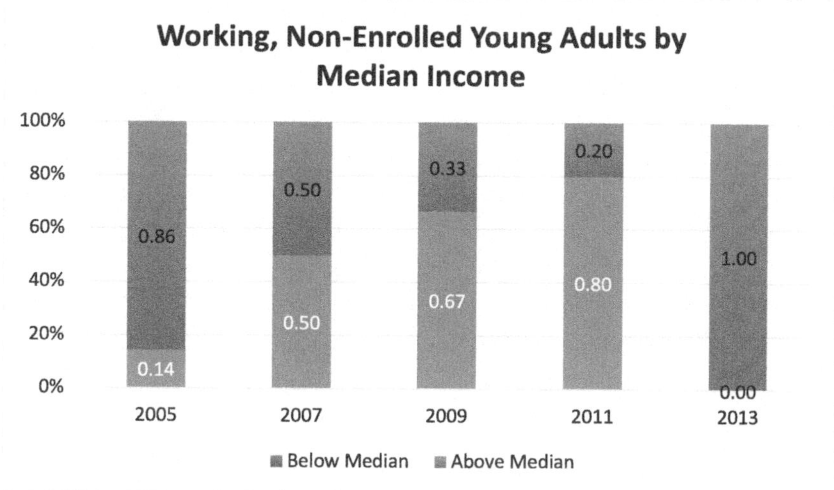

Figure 5.6 Working Young Adults by Income Group

Source: Panel Study of Income Dynamics, public use dataset (2017). Produced and distributed by the Survey Research Center, Institute for Social Research, University of Michigan, Ann Arbor, MI.

Note: Author analysis of data

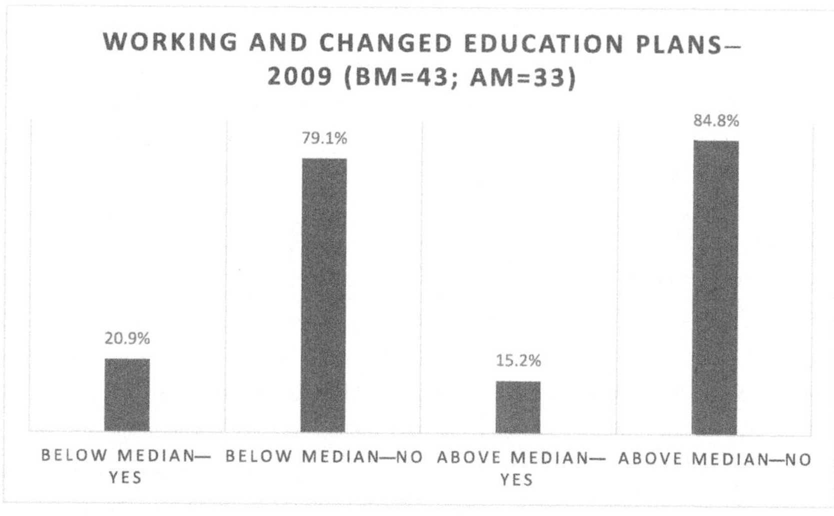

Figure 5.7 Working Young Adults Who Changed Education Plans—2009

Source: Panel Study of Income Dynamics, public use dataset (2017). Produced and distributed by the Survey Research Center, Institute for Social Research, University of Michigan, Ann Arbor, MI.

Note: Author analysis of data

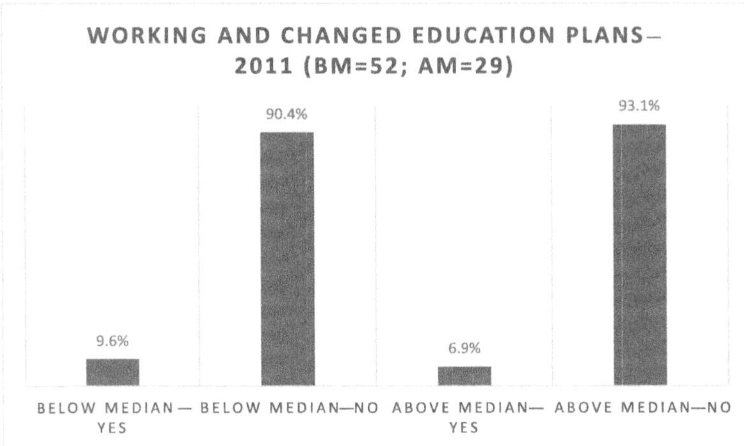

Figure 5.8 Working Young Adults Who Changed Education Plans—2011

Source: Panel Study of Income Dynamics, public use dataset (2017). Produced and distributed by the Survey Research Center, Institute for Social Research, University of Michigan, Ann Arbor, MI.

Note: Author analysis of data

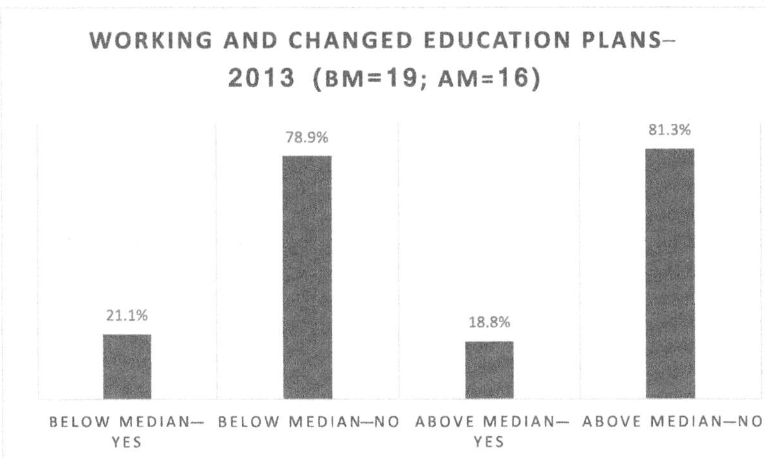

Figure 5.9 Working Young Adults Who Changed Education Plans—2013

Source: Panel Study of Income Dynamics, public use dataset (2017). Produced and distributed by the Survey Research Center, Institute for Social Research, University of Michigan, Ann Arbor, MI.

Note: Author analysis of data

perhaps an inclination to explore postsecondary education among less resourced persons during this shock period.

The descriptive data highlight differences in patterns of enrolled young adults across above-median- and below-median-income groups, with a brief review of the education planning among young adults who were working and not enrolled. The next set of findings highlights the primary group of interest for the research questions, enrolled young adults, and assesses the statistical significance of differences in enrollment and education planning changes among below median income and above median income, enrolled and working, young adults.

Enrollment Pattern Differences. Table 5.1 summarizes enrollment patterns across the survey years under study: 2005, 2007, 2009, 2011, and 2013. In each of the survey years, the difference between below- and above-median-income young adults in their enrollment patterns is statistically significant ($p < .05$), supporting the conclusions identified in the summary of descriptive statistics that below-median-income students enrolled at a lower rate than their above-median counterparts. The most significant differences are observed in 2007, 2009, 2011, and 2013.

In reporting the effect of the Great Recession on education plans, the chi-square tests only show a statistically significant difference in the economic shock's impact on the education planning of below-median-income and above-median-income students in 2011, with 2009 and 2013 not showing a significant difference. This finding also aligns with the general population increase in enrollment as the Great Recession presented in earlier chapters, with this group of PSID young adults across both income categories maintaining a steady pace of enrollment, peaking during the shock. For those who changed their education plans, Table 5.2 provides a summary of these findings.

Table 5.1 Postsecondary Enrollment of Above-Median-Income and Below-Median-Income Young Adults (Percent)

Cohort	*Above-Median Income (Percent)*	*Below-Median Income (Percent)*
2005*	83.3	72.9
2007***	83.9	63.9
2009***	88.0	74.2
2011***	88.6	68.1
2013***	86.8	66.9

*P ≤ 0.05; **P ≤ 0.01; ***P ≤ 0.001

Source: Panel Study of Income Dynamics, public use dataset (2017). Produced and distributed by the Survey Research Center, Institute for Social Research, University of Michigan, Ann Arbor, MI.

Note: Author analysis of data

Table 5.2 Above-Median-Income and Below-Median-Income Enrolled Young Adults Who Changed Their Education Plans Because of the Great Recession (Percent)

Cohort	*Above-Median Income (Percent)*	*Below-Median Income (Percent)*
2009	15.7	25.0
2011**	18.5	31.3
2013	9.9	17.6

*P ≤ 0.05; **P ≤ 0.01; ***P ≤ 0.001

Source: Panel Study of Income Dynamics, public use dataset (2017). Produced and distributed by the Survey Research Center, Institute for Social Research, University of Michigan, Ann Arbor, MI.

Note: Author analysis of data

For working, non-enrolled young adults who reported that the Great Recession caused them to change their education plans, no statistically significant difference could be determined between above-median-income and below-median-income young adults. The number of respondents falling in these categories (i.e., only working; changed education plans) was zero (2009: n = 0; 2011: n = 0; 2013: n = 0).

In sum, the PSID dataset affirms the presence of effects of the Great Recession on postsecondary education enrollment and planning for enrolled and working young adults across below-median and above-median incomes. Across above- and below-median incomes, enrollment in postsecondary education increased between 2005 and 2011, and then dropped by 2013, four years after the Great Recession was declared over. Additionally, among those in this group who stated that the Great Recession caused them to change their education plans (25 percent in 2009, 31 percent in 2011, and 18 percent in 2013), neither dropping out of school nor postponing education was reported as a change they would pursue. However, it is only in 2011 where statistically significant differences in education planning between income groups are observed. In terms of working young adults, below-median young adults were the majority of respondents who were working for all but one (2013) of the survey years. The 2009 survey had the highest proportion of respondents in this group, reporting they would change their education plans; this same pattern played out for above-median respondents in 2009 as well. For below-median, working, non-enrolled young adults, the Great Recession had no impact on their education planning across the three cohorts that reported on this question; only one above-median income, working, non-enrolled young adult stated that the Great Recession altered their education plans.

As noted earlier, while enrolled participants reported changing major as a common choice, across both income groups, the most frequently reported action taken to change education plans was "Other." This data point indicated additional education decision drivers at work that were not accounted for among the response categories offered. It is this finding that opened the question of what factors were under-specified in the PSID-TA that could be investigated through phenomenological interviews. The qualitative component enabled deeper insights on the meaning making processes during the postsecondary period critical to identity development for diverse young adults.

Qualitative Interview Themes and Findings

The phenomenological interviews facilitated investigating the shock impact on postsecondary education planning in real time. This study component addressed the third study research question:

- Eleven years after the Great Recession ended, have there been ***any changes in the key factors that inform education planning*** for young adults between the ages of 18 and 20?

The participant pool sustains the study's focus on enrolled 18- to 20-year olds established in the quantitative component, with particular interest in shock impacts on their postsecondary enrollment planning and experiences not captured in the PSID survey. The interview protocol was structured to explore participant experiences and meaning making processes occurring during the COVID-19 shock. It permitted determination of themes that overlapped with findings in the PSID survey data, while also surfacing unknown aspects of the spectrum of shock-related changes made to postsecondary education and work plans. Further, the interview data makes possible discernment of identity development processes that are driven by individuals' assessment of risks, challenges and supports.

Participant interviews were carried out in the U.S. in Spring, 2021, at the height of the COVID-19 global pandemic and a COVID-19 triggered recession (see Chapter 1). One year earlier, the U.S. had undergone a societal racial reckoning when Mr. George Floyd, an African-American man, was brutally murdered by police on a public street in full daylight. The tragic incident was recorded on video and dominated air waves and social media, shocking a nation already reeling from the traumatic effects of the pandemic's lethal effects. For the African American community in the U.S. it was a particularly difficult moment to endure. The harrowing images of his torturous death and the recording of Mr. Floyd's visceral call for his mother when his suffering was at its worst seemed to cut through any psychic protective membrane so many African Americans cultivate to navigate life in the U.S. It was a clear reminder that African Americans faced exposure to two lethal pathogens, the biologically-based COVID virus and unaddressed racism, with no solution for either in sight. It was at that time that the Black Lives Matter movement called out the grave reality of endemic racial inequality in the U.S. The grass roots movement opened the floodgates for a unified, transracial call for justice and equity. In that moment, the protests forced U.S. society in particular to face the unresolved, tragic conundrum: the promises set forth in the country's founding documents that prioritized freedom and equality interacted with systems that consistently drove unequal outcomes at the group and population levels (e.g., disparate rates of household income and employment recovery by race and ethnicity after the Great Recession) despite individual effort, especially for persons of color as well as those from less-resourced backgrounds. This nationwide movement became global, piercing the malaise of COVID-induced anxiety with a clear awareness of the cost of unaddressed racial and ethnic hate, inequality, and discrimination in all its forms. Additional movements gained momentum during this time—such as StopAsianHate, Trans Rights, MeToo, Indigenous and First Nation rights, immigrant rights, environmental justice, and the climate crisis. They emerged to push back against a status quo that refused to acknowledge or address the needs and interests of diverse groups. The protests were effective in establishing the local-national-global linkages of systemic issues, underscoring the interconnected and intersectional nature of threats, with the lowest resourced and most vulnerable enduring the most egregious effects.

The rise of social movements during COVID, then, put a spotlight on how the lack of responsiveness to systemic and environmental harms constituted its own form of violence, with consequences that were not hypothetical but actualized and many times lethal.

In sum, the COVID-19 pandemic inexorably disrupted the notion that the status quo was working fine for all: When the rhythm of life halted, the realization of imminent threat to one's mortality was unavoidable. It was during this period, which was also rife with rampant misinformation emanating from elected leaders and their surrogates within and outside of government, that many individuals, organizations, and institutions seized the moment of clarity to re-orient their priorities to engage enduring issues of inequality. It was no longer a question of whether and which humans were vulnerable; it was now a question of the degreee of the interconnected nature of vulnerability and how to move forward. These events also challenged research, social services, and policy-making institutions to discern and ameliorate the immediate and enduring harms from the pandemic shock, testing new strategies, and tactics. New initiatives emerged to engage immediate human need (e.g., a federal moratorium on evictions was mandated to avoid further loss of homes [Centers for Disease Control, 2020]). Social science research that studied human beings solely in terms of their market utility was ill-prepared to engage the human toll and realities of this public health emergency colliding with endemic inequality. Certainly, amid these COVID-era movements, the underlying dynamics of human development and identity development surged to the fore necessitating new context sensitive, human-centered research and policy approaches that acknowledged diverse young adult experiences in the 21st century. It is in this context that the phenomenological qualitative interviews were conducted.

This component of the human development theoretically-based study was launched to address the knowledge gap on shock-period identity development processes by examining the postsecondary experiences of young adults eleven years after the Great Recession, which coincided with the COVID-19 pandemic. The interview data captured in-the-moment perspectives from a diverse group of young adults regarding effects of the shock, building on insights from the study of the effects of the Great Recession on education planning for 18- to 20-year-old young adults. The interview protocol was designed to explore individuals' reflections on how they assessed risks, understood and accessed supports, and made sense of their education plans and goals as they navigated living and learning conditions inexorably altered by the shock.

The COVID-19 public health advisories to avoid in-person contact to minimize the aggressive spread of the lethal virus resulted in the closure of postsecondary institutions in Spring 2020. Those institutions that did remain open provided restricted access to authorized, essential personnel and enrolled students only. As such, in-person interviews with students at their campuses were not possible. Therefore, all institutional and participant recruitment activities, which included undergoing IRB review at participating postsecondary institutions, were carried out through email and over the internet.

The author conducted interviews over the internet utilizing a commonly used web conference program, which presented certain methodological challenges (e.g., stability of internet connections; ensuring participants were empowered to secure safe, private location for interviews that suited their confidentiality needs) and advantages (i.e., expanded the geographic range of the recruitment pool with the study notices distributed nationally). As such, the study methods strictly adhered to standardized steps for scheduling and protocol administration to minimize variability in data collection. This included affirming that participants and the author utilized the same web conference system to ensure uniformity of key features and functionality in the online interview session environment (e.g., participants' ability to opt-out of the interview at any point, the author conducting interviews from the same location, with both audio and video activated throughout each participant session, sustaining visual and audio continuity across all interviews). The resulting participant pool was comprised of racially, ethnically, and geographically diverse young adults attending public and private, 2- and 4-year institutions. In addition to demographic and enrollment information, many participants volunteered additional detail on their backgrounds, including first-generation college attendance and immigrant statuses. All individuals were generous with their time and provided candid, invaluable insights on their life experiences during the COVID-19 pandemic shock.

Figure 5.10 presents a summary of key themes, organized by interview protocol section, that emerged from the interviews. The primary research questions regarding changes to education plans because of the pandemic and recession shock surfaced participant experiences that were affirmative of the Great Recession findings presented earlier in the chapter: The vast majority of participants reported not changing their plans. Among diverse young adults who reported they changed education plans because of the shock, they cited changing their academic major or reconceptualizing their education and work goals. Further exploration of participants' impressions of risks and challenges they faced in realizing their education and work plans permitted assessment of meaning making processes at work. Here, participants conveyed concerns about meeting financial obligations, feeling disconnected from their peers and institutions, and challenges maintaining focus in online learning environments. There was also a discernment of the ramifications of altered institutional contexts and how to attain reliable information regarding their course of study, internships, and staging future job prospects amid economic and public health precarity. Through this, there was an overall consensus regarding the active presence and salutary effects of key supports. Indeed, across the resource levels designated by participants—highly-resourced, mid-resourced, or low-resourced—all reported being sufficiently resourced to meet their needs and consistently conveyed a commitment to their postsecondary education in the midst of the COVID-19 shock.

Next, a detailed presentation of participants' remarks illustrates the key themes summarized in Figure 5.10. The names of young adults are pseudonyms,

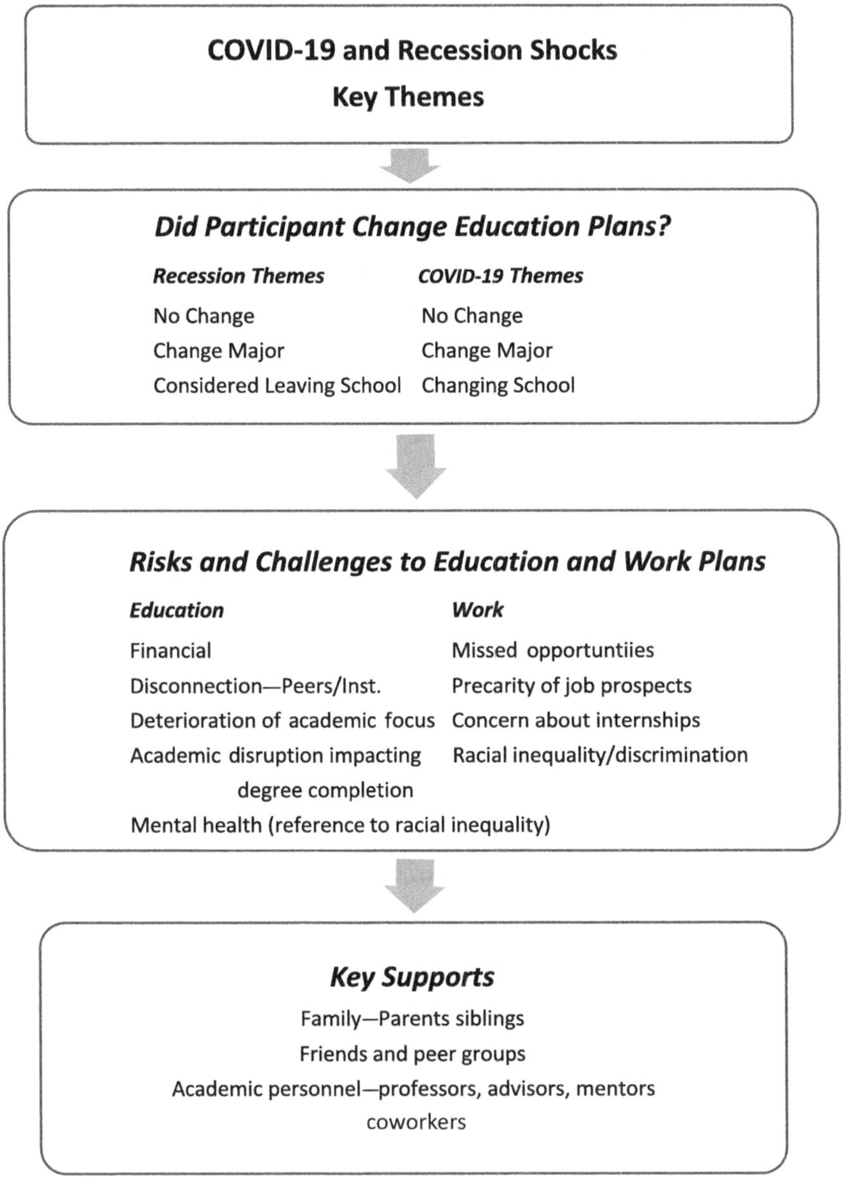

Figure 5.10 Qualitative Interview Themes

with demographic references (gender, race, and ethnic identities) reported as described by participants. The protocol utilized for the interviews (see Appendix) facilitated a conversational interview, ensuring a seamless flow of discussion and allowing for participants to pursue lines of thinking and reflection as they emerged as they responded to questions. While a departure from the original study design, which assumed in-person interviews, the online interview setting did not present any technical barrier to participants who screened into the study. Participants progressed through the questions easily, picking up their line of thought in the rare instances where interruptions occurred, owed either to lost internet connectivity or other disturbances where they were located. (It should be noted that contemporaneous notes captured during all interviews helped to sustain lines of inquiry, and these proved helpful guiding respondents back to the conversational thread underway at the time of an inadvertent interruption.) Indeed, most study participants conveyed a high level of comfort with being interviewed online, perhaps aided in large part by the ongoing engagement with and extensive use of virtual tools for coursework, effectively priming participants for a virtual interview context. Further, during the gaining cooperation phase, participants were encouraged to identify interview locations that met their particular privacy needs. Prompting and probing occurred when students referenced terms of art or concepts that were either unclear or where clarification from participants would ensure accuracy in the interpretation of their intended meaning.

The tone of the remarks presented in this chapter, then, conveys candor and in-the-moment discernment, revealing how participants experienced the global pandemic shock as they made meaning of their work and education goals while living amid shock-related challenges and constraints. Indeed, these young adults' responses and reflections convey the complexity and nuances of enrolled young adult experiences as they made meaning of their paths during an historic public health and recessionary shock. Their commonality in their shared experience of living and learning under COVID-19 restrictions is all the more interesting given the broad spectrum of their reported major fields of study. These broad categories, along with subfield emphases, are enumerated below and give a good sense of the range of interests held by the study participants:

Science, Technology, Engineering and Mathematics (STEM):

Computer Science, Information Technology, Biochemistry, Environmental Engineering, Engineering

Social Sciences:

Pscyhology, International Relations

Humanities:

Women's and Gender Studies

Business:

International Business, Accounting, Finance

Whether these subject area interests were prospective (a few first-year students reported that their institutions did not permit formal major declarations in the first year), newly-declared or established, these participants' broad range of interests were demonstrative of an ambitious agenda for their futures.

It is critical to acknowledge that the interviews occurred at a time when the COVID-19 virus infection rate was at a new peak nationally. As the interviewer who was also enrolled in a postsecondary institution, I was existing under the same COVID-19 remote working and public health advisories as the participants. As such, I was able to bring to the interviews a heightened sensitivity to the difficulties and confusions associated with pursuing education during pandemic precipitated by a novel virus. Indeed, the sustained engagement of the research study, with support from institutions and organizations, provided an added sense of purpose for pursuing this research in the moment to garner critical insights that might support student success by better understanding their challenges.

The Role of Education During a Shock—An Enduring Positive

> It gives me, definitely, I would say an opportunity to move up in the classes of America. So I would say currently I was growing up in I'd say lower middle-class, but I would see that with education I could move up in the higher middle-class of America. And it'll give me an opportunity to, like, better be stable financially compared to my parents which is something I really want to get geared to and hopefully be able to support them with their financial problems as I graduate and get myself situated with a career, hopefully.
>
> Martin, First-Generation College Junior

Among the first questions posed in the interview was one that asked that participants explain the role a college education plays in where they want to go in life. The response to this question allowed for establishing an interview approach and follow-up prompts anchored in how participants described how they were oriented to their college education. This, then, helped ensure the participants' own perceptions and expectations of a college education in their lives framed the interview approach, further anchoring the subject of postsecondary education within the study's phenomenological interview approach.

All participants were unanimous in their positive assessment of a college education, citing the central role it plays in achieving their goals. This transcended first-generation enrollment status, major field of study as well as demographic characteristics reported by participants (i.e., race/ethnicity, immigration status, gender identity). The participants noted the acquisition of academic, professional, and life skills that would prepare them for success after college in their chosen professions and beyond.

In providing these insights, they also shared identity affirming benefits of the college degree attainment. Exemplified by Holly, who is discussed later in the chapter, provides a response to the question of the role of a college education and its validation of professional legitimacy:

> I am interested in entering like the bigger companies like [two large private sector companies] as like a software engineer, and especially as a woman I'd have to have, like, you know, the degree to prove, you know, I'm worth it . . . To say that I'm worth it, it means, like, I had the proper education because there are some software engineers who just went to boot camps or taught themselves, but they lack the foundation, the knowledge in that field. And I feel like having that, and having proof of it would just, you know, kind of put me, like, a better chance above the rest.

Robert explained the developmental function of college in preparing for adulthood, stating:

> It [a college education] plays, for me, a very necessary role in that I learn, basically, it's both actual education and, like, you know, the major I want to pursue in, but also I feel like a training ground on how to be an adult.
>
> Interviewer: Interesting. Could you say a little bit more about what it means to be an adult; what that means?
>
> Taking in responsibilities, learning to know what's a priority and what's not knowing how to manage time, knowing what you need to do to take care of yourself, you know, learning to live with a person that's basically your equal and not your parents.

It is the identity development attributes of postsecondary education pursuits during shocks that are of interest for this component of the study. Throughout the course of the interviews, participants varied in the detail provided, at times revisiting earlier responses to either refine or elaborate on a particular topic. Overall, their thoughtfulness and generosity of time conveyed a clear commitment to providing accurate and useful responses that would contribute vital data for understanding their experiences and the nature of the impact of shocks more broadly.

Change in Education Plans

The interview explored how the pandemic shock, and linked recession, caused participants to make adjustments to their education plans. This construct was explored by posing the following questions to participants:

Has the current pandemic caused you to change your education plans? (if yes: How is that?)
Has the current recession caused you to change your education plans? (if yes: How is that?)

Nearly all participants responding to these two questions shared that the current recession did not change their education plans (n = 15), while nearly half of participants (n = 8) shared that pandemic had an effect. In describing why the recession did not impact his education, Engineer Management major Jason, who was a sophomore enrolled at a four-year private institution, noted that his scholarship program provided critical stability in the midst of economic uncertainty, with an awareness that it was essential to his ability to remain enrolled:

> Well, I go to school now because of a scholarship, so personally as long as the scholarship is still on, like, it hasn't really changed my education plans, I'm still planning on graduating in two years.

Another participant, Daphne, explicitly shared that the recession caused changes to her education plans, indicating that the economic precarity of the recession might result in dropping out of college or revising her life goals. A psychology major who was enrolled and working, she shared possibly shifting to an "entrepreneurial path" to increase earning potential in her professional pursuits:

> I guess the current economic status of America today is making me re-question whether education is really high priority because everything is kind of on pause. It's making me, I guess, there is really no guarantee right now. We're kind of living on a day-to-day basis, so I feel like my gears have shifted towards more so money and just survival, honestly, and that is this whole, like, state of America today. It's kind of making me put my education on the back end because of that. If that makes sense?
>
> Interviewer: Yeah, so when you say, "on the back end," what do you mean by that?
>
> I guess lower in priority. Like I'm only taking two classes right now and I'm thinking to take a semester off, next semester, to just kind of renegotiate my financial wellness, I guess.

Among those who answered "Yes" to the question "Has the current pandemic caused you to change your education plans," respondents primarily shared adaptations they were making in order to attend their courses remotely over the internet. One participant succinctly expressed how online learning was not ideal:

> [E]verything changed like with the virtual classes, like right now the classes are really strange and that make us – I feel like all students feel like uncomfortable.

This was also in the midst of adapting to institutional challenges sharing information in order to meet the needs of their individual students' education plans. For first-year students, how participants were oriented to an institution played a role in their sense of self-efficacy navigating postsecondary education contexts.

Referenced earlier, Jason, a Hispanic male in his sophomore year in college majoring in Engineer Management, had resumed in-person classes. He also enjoyed his job working as a part-time soccer coach. Jason shared that his college scholarship played a significant role in minimizing the effects of the recession on his education. ("Well I go to school now because of a scholarship, so personally as long as the scholarship is still on, like, it hasn't really changed my education plans, I'm still planning on graduating in two years."). The pandemic sharpened his focus on the connection between his future career goals. Building on knowledge gained and maturation developed during his freshman year, he prioritized improving his academic performance while strengthening his professional network for his career:

> Yeah, so I've added – as a freshman – well, personally, whenever you start in college as a freshman you kind of like don't know what you're getting into, so you kind of just start everything out and you're kind of like seeing, browsing different things. Even when I came to the college, like I knew what I wanted to be, I wanted to be something in engineering. So I was like now after that pandemic hit, like I completely made my focus into management, engineering management . . . just adding more focus like in terms of asking questions making sure that I'm doing the right thing so that I can better prepare so whenever I graduate, I could secure a job or a career in the field. But I would say that my focus has increased by me being more involved in asking anything related to my career; anything related like professors, advisors, even students, upper-class students. So, before the pandemic I was just coming to school, I was doing my work, I was doing the necessary stuff to keep good grades and everything, but I wasn't really focused as I would say, per se, I wasn't invested in my career.

Jason continued that his heightened focus included not just expanding his network of academic and professional support but also considerations of shifting his major to possibly identify a "shock-proof" career choice:

> It [The pandemic] hasn't necessarily changed my education plans, it has made sure that I choose the correct – cause seeing the pandemic, seeing how it has affected some people has made me realize whether what major I should do that won't affect me if something was to happen in the future. Whether my stability in the job in whatever job I get, or career, is still intact no matter if a pandemic hits or something. So it hasn't necessarily changed my educational plans, but I've had more focus, like it's added focus to my plans.

The theme of changing major was dominant among participants who reported changing their education plans. Robert was attending community college as a second-year psychology student with an online freelance job as a captionist. He identified as Asian/Pacific Islander and shared that he was considering changing his major, moving from a course of study in the sciences to law because of ongoing social issues, particularly associated with the broad social reckoning with racial inequality and hatred. These factors combined caused him to seriously consider how he could make a more significant contribution to society:

> I think initially I wanted to go through the sciences, but with everything going on I've been thinking about pursuing the justice system, like maybe go into business law or something, like pursue some sort of business major. Just with a bit of reflection and just seeing how the news and society lately, I just thought maybe there's something bigger I can do for the whole of society in some way.

For Jason and Robert, then, the shock brought about a deeper awareness of how their education paths were consequential not just to their professions. For Robert especially, it had an inextricable link to how he considered his own agency in shaping and improving society through his chosen profession.

Ana's experience as a freshman picks up on themes noted by Jason about the developmental function of the first year of college and lessons learned from missteps. Ana was a freshman at a four-year public university, intended to major in business and architecture. A Mexican American woman, she also earned money running an online shop full time. In fact, she was happy to share a link with the interviewer, conveying a clear sense of pride in her burgeoning business venture. She participated in her interview from her residence where she attended her online courses. During the interview, she expressed regret about the lost opportunities of launching her college career online and the less-than-ideal circumstances surrounding her orientation to her institution. She encountered struggles with online events that replaced in-person orientation events, impeding her ability to establish social connections at the start of her college career.

> Maybe if I had gone to [university orientation event] or any of the [four year public university] events, I would have known that, but I couldn't go, so I guess that's another – I was really sad that I couldn't go to [university orientation event] because that's a day that everyone talks about, like, "Oh, [university orientation event]." Like, you get to know, like, everyone you see on campus. Like it's – I don't know, that's something that this pandemic has stolen from me.

Initially, Ana provided a seemingly contradictory response, first answering "No" to the question of whether the pandemic caused her to change her education plans, then providing additional detail on her educational journey in a pandemic context. She shared that the lack of in-person instruction and counseling support during COVID-19 closures complicated her path toward meeting course requirements.

> No . . . But I mean if you could consider, like, dropping classes because of, like, just – so I honestly think I would have succeeded a lot more in my classes had this been in-person. You know, I did have to drop some classes last semester that I probably could have maintained had this – had I been in person with my professors and collaborating with my peers, but that's probably the only change that I've experienced in terms of the pandemic.
>
> Last year in the fall I was taking [course name], which is intro to business, which is a prerequisite for the [subject] major but I dropped it and decided to take it this semester because I couldn't handle it – I just couldn't handle it with my other classes, so I had to drop it. And I don't think I would have had to had I had more support.

Ana's comments portray a visceral experience of loss and confusion navigating the first year of college remotely along with struggles finding and building a supportive peer network. For Ana, it resulted in adjusting her planned course of study and having a more circuitous journey to her intended field of study.

Jessica, an Information Technology major working at the school newspaper, was also living at home like Ana and was quarantining with her parents and grandmother at the time of the interview. An African American woman in her freshman year at a community college, the change in her education plans was both strategic and institution focused, informed by COVID-19 more than recessionary conditions. She described her decision to switch from her planned entry into a four-year college to a two-year community college:

> No, the current recession hasn't caused me to change my educational plans. I would say that COVID pretty much caused me to change my education plan

> because COVID started during my senior of high school [in 2020] and I was originally thinking about either going to a four-year school like [public university] or like I was thinking about [private university], so I'm considering it, but I had decided just with everything that was going on it might just be best to just go to community college because I wasn't going to be able to get the full college experience, so why pay the full four-years? I'm not going to be able to, like, really enjoy it.

Natalia was a third-year International Business major at a private four-year college who lived at home with her parents during the COVID pandemic. She came to the U.S. with her parents when she was six years old and owed her independent, self-starter personality to her experiences spanning back to second grade:

> It was hard at the beginning. But when I was in Mexico, I took bilingual classes. So, when I was six, and I started second grade here in the U.S., I was not behind . . . But it was still hard because my parents didn't speak English, so it was on me . . . But I'm actually glad because it just made me more independent at a young [age].

An only child, she relayed that she enjoyed a very close relationship with her parents and relied on their counsel. As a college freshman she had been selected to represent her school at a prestigious convening, surprising herself that she was able to navigate the pressures of learning a new context and how to present herself to other campus representatives. She succeeded on all fronts, winning an award based on her performance.

> I was able to attend the . . . intercollegiate state legislative conference that was held in [location], and I was a head delegate for [institution] as a freshman. So, I thought that it was very important because there I was able to socialize with students from across the state of [state name], and it was like the first time that I had ever done something like that—and, being a freshman too, being the leader. So, that really helped me to—basically, I really learned leadership skills and how to communicate better with people from different backgrounds and different cultures, and that's just something that really helped me as well . . .

It was an experience that was a source of pride and provided her with a confidence that opened up new possibilities in her awareness of her own potential to be successful in new undertakings. Her capacity to cope with the pandemic's disruptions seemed linked to those experiences navigating challenges and new experiences. When asked if the pandemic impacted her education plans, Natalia stated:

> Not really. And the reason is because I keep an agenda with me, and I write all of my homework down and everything that I have to do that day and I make

sure that, by the end of the day, I have everything accomplished. So, even if I have a class online, I make that more a priority because I know that I'm going to have to pay more attention, and it's going to demand more time. So, yeah. But I'm doing well in all of my classes, yes.

[T]he reason why I feel that that pandemic has not really affected my education is because ever since I was little, I was really independent, but I could understand how other students are struggling right now because they have always relied on being in person, and sometimes it's not easy to be flexible and especially, I understand that it's harder for those students that have jobs to do well in school because time management is just really important. You really need to make use of their time—especially if they're working, because I know some of my friends work full-time while they're in school, and it can be really hard.

Alan, a college freshman majoring in Computer Science, also came to the U.S. as a child with his family. He was close to his brother and parents who emigrated from Vietnam. In fact, in college Alan gained renewed interested in exploring his Vietnamese identity and heritage, planning to major in Asian Studies. While he was excited about connecting to his Vietnamese identity, he encountered dissonance in engaging Vietnamese culture as an academic subject. He stated:

[I]n the Asian studies department we have a lot of professors that, to be frank, they're like White, like they're predominantly White professors, and even though they're super sweet, right, sometimes I feel like the content they're giving us is disconnected to what I am trying to get at here cause, like I guess like I took a class about Vietnam and I was hoping to learn, like, oh, the Vietnamese, like, identity, like the culture behind like the holidays and the festivals, and I think what I got more was a Western view of Vietnam and looking at Vietnam in the bigger scale; right? It was like trying to – it was like the study was trying to decipher what the Vietnamese wanted, but, like, you know, that's looking to the history. Like they're looking – because like I guess Vietnam as a country, we're not as dominant, like, a lot of our history has been like other countries taking over us and then, like, switching back and forth and whatnot, and so that was like the view; right? Like how did the people outside – like how did the foreigners affect Vietnam basically, and it's like trying to decipher but I think, I guess, that's like really – it's just a different focus and honestly, I just wanted to know what Vietnamese identity was.

When discussing his educational experiences more broadly, Alan noted that the uncertainty raised by COVID-19 restrictions disrupted his assumptions about the standard timing of pursuing enrichment opportunities, such as study abroad.

It imbued him with a sense of urgency to take advantage of horizon-expanding opportunities available to him:

> Yeah, I think, like, just me being more conscious of the time that I have left because . . . like, with the pandemic, I mean, it basically says like studying abroad in college, like, sophomore year, like coming up next year, would be sort of, like, dangerous – or not dangerous but we don't really know what's happening next year, and then like what's going to happen junior and senior year, so I'm sort of, like, the thoughts about career, it's kind of in the back now because I really want to take any opportunity I can to study abroad, like, in junior and senior year. If that's, like, the decision between, like, getting internship at, like, [large software company] or, like, studying abroad in Spain where – because, like, I have to take any opportunity, so now just being more conscious about, like, what non-job opportunity I'm willing to take, yeah.

Risks or Challenges to Achieving Education Goals

The cultivation of effective coping strategies emerges through encountering and overcoming risks and challenges, a process that is augmented and aided by the presence of supports, or protective factors. The interview protocol, then, delved into participants' descriptions of risks and challenges.

What are the top three risks or challenges to achieving your education goals right now? (Answering "None" is an acceptable response)

Financial concerns were the most dominant theme related to education risks or challenges, cited by participants across high, medium, and low resource levels and institution type. Crystal, a medium-resourced African American female freshman majoring in Computer Science at a public four-year institution with hopes to start a career in the tech industry, Robert, a second-year community college student majoring in Psychology referenced earlier, and James, a Business major in his first year attending a private four-year private institution who came to study in the U.S. from a country in Sub-Saharan Africa and identified as low-resourced, all noted financial concerns.

> School is very expensive; I don't want [to go] to graduate school with loans, so finding like scholarships, I'm applying to them and, like, getting them, that's a challenge for me and kind of a big stressor.—Crystal
>
> . . . it's probably financial issues cause, you know, high tuition because this is really expensive here.—Robert

> And apart from choosing the wrong major, some financial risks could also come into play, because college is about—whether anybody likes it or not, college is about money. It's about spending money and to be able to make money in the future —James.

In discussing financial concerns, some placed the risk in the context of broader familial responsibilities they felt, like Alan did. He mentioned wanting to alleviate the pressure on his parents and noted the implications for pursuing graduate study after college:

> I think, so the number one risk is definitely like coming to reality, like, since I'm low income, I have to, like, at first, I have to somewhat make money for my family and even if, like, even if they tell me it's perfectly fine, like, "We'll pay for your college and we'll pay for whatever is coming up." I don't think it's right, so I just ignore what my parents try to tell me and like I think about how I'm going to pay for my own college cause I'm not going to let them pay. So, I have to come to reality, like, I think pursuing academia, like pursuing a PhD right out of college is something I'm really scared about cause I don't know how feasible that is."

Another recurring theme that emerged centered around issues and challenges associated with online learning due to COVID-related restrictions on in-person instruction, echoing Ana's description of changes she made to her education plans. Participants described a feeling of disconnectedness and loss of their full on-campus experience of being a college student as well as difficulty focusing on their studies. David, majoring in Accounting in his junior (third) year, was actually attending classes on campus at the time of his interview. An African American man with a strong interest in physics and astrology, he went to live with his father after his mother passed away, then returned to his home city to finish high school before traveling across the country to attend college. He emphasized the difficulty with avoiding distractions and investigated strategies to remain focused on his studies in an online learning context, lamenting the lost "good old days" of using paper-based books:

> Well distractions I'm referring to is just a lot of it, like, electronic stuff in general, like, you know, [social media tool], video games, just things like that, and even having a computer in general because, you know, back in the day when it was mostly books and stuff, people – it was easier for people to memorize stuff. I read on [search engine] that it's easier to retain information when you're reading something rather than when you're looking at it on a computer because it's something to do with, like, the feel of the book, you

> actually flipping the pages, it just helps out, so, you know, people back then didn't have that luxury as we do now. Online you can find any book ever, so it's just . . . well, I guess more stuff to do.

Ana understood that her learning style would be best served through social ties and building community with fellow students to build mutually reinforcing accountability frameworks in schoolwork. The lack of in-person contact made socializing and making friends more difficult for her to stay on track with online learning:

> Well I think that, like, finding – okay, so I haven't really made a lot of friends. I've only made, like, three, and I try to make friends, but no one seems to really be in the mood for talking, so I think having someone – or at least like a person that I know in the class would be extremely helpful, like, "Hey, let's study together. Hey, let's motivate each other to go to class." Because it's easy to not want to go to class and it's – like my class is at 8:00 a.m. every day – no – yeah, every day for business – or it was. And I'm taking it this semester, but it's hard to want to get up and resist the temptation to just watch the recording later. But that messed me up last semester. And, yeah, I learned my lesson.

While Ana shared these remarks in the context of changes to her education plans caused by COVID-19, she highlights academic risks emanating from lost social connections and camaraderie with her fellow freshman students. Jessica elaborated on challenges collaborating with her classmates:

> I would probably say the second risk is probably the fact that due to this sort of communication barrier, it is a little more difficult for me to sort of reach out and collaborate with my fellow classmates. Like we have group projects but it's sort of like entirely online and we're texting each other back and forth, but we each have our own different schedules because some people work and, you know, some people have children, so it's sort of difficult to sort of find people who are able to allocate time for us, to just sort of meet up and do, you know, assignments. At least it's like when everybody is at the college you know that everybody has time . . .

This experience aligns with findings from a study examining the challenges of implementing online learning during COVID-19 shutdowns (García-Morales, Garrido-Morreno, & Martín-Rojas, 2021). The researchers cite findings in which students report "boredom, sense of isolation, lack of time to follow the different subjects and lack of self-organizing capabilities" (*Ibid*, p. 3).

Mental health was also referenced as a risk that was a struggle, with students sharing both negative and positive experiences securing supports that engaged their mental health needs. Daphne was in her first year as a Psychology major at community college who was employed at a nearby store at the time of the interview. As referenced earlier, she had considered dropping out of college for a time due to concerns about achieving her education and work goals owed to risks linked to inequality in the U.S. She noted the tensions of working and going to school, along with the challenges of overcoming inequality as a woman and a person of color in the U.S. (she described her racial/ethnic affiliation as Asian) with implications for her mental health when describing challenges to her education goals:

> Second one [risk or challenge] would be inequality in many different ways, you know? Like being a woman, being a person of color even I struggle with mental health. I feel like those things definitely make it harder for me to pursue the same education another person might pursue being in like a different subset of whatever.

Holly, enrolled in a four-year private college and identified as West Asian-Kurdish, relied on her friends for support but also shared that taking care of her mental health as a key risk she shared with her fellow students:

> Like I feel like my mental health has definitely deteriorated a little bit more because of like the pressure of college. I think that's probably the only risk I can think of is just like my mental health. It's – you know a very common thing I have noticed among college students.

Risks or Challenges to Achieving Work Goals

Remaining within the broad topic of risks and challenges, the interview then inquired about respondents' description of risks or challenges achieving their work goals as experienced at the time of the interview. The key question was as follows:

What are the top three risks or challenges to achieving your work goals right now? (Answering "None" is an acceptable response).

The primary themes identified by study participants revealed concerns about possible missed opportunities to pursue their intended career paths. It is important to note that over half of the participants reported being both enrolled and working, further emphasizing the negotiation of multiple roles at the time of the interviews. Only one of the participants reported having a job related to the career they intended to pursue after graduation. Overall, participants related challenges unique to the COVID-19 shock, citing obstacles to obtaining crucial internships while they were enrolled in school that could lead to job offers after college, the precarity of the job market they will encounter, and related financial concerns. Martin, a 20-year-old, Mexican American male majoring in Environmental Engineering at a four-year public university shared:

> [A] lot of the big worries that I have in college right now is getting an internship for during one of these summers while I'm in college. A lot of people have told me and career advisors like really push on the idea of getting an internship before you graduate from college because they say it'll really boost your chances of landing a job right after college. So that's a big one right now is trying to get an internship. Last year—last summer, I believe—, I was able to get an internship but because of the pandemic it was canceled, so I was like really, really let down by that. So hopefully we're still able to – or the pandemic ends, and I can get one and that'll like alleviate some of my worries of not being able to get an internship because it's a big worry.
>
> Like not getting an internship after college I'm kind of worried like it'll be hard to get a job in the engineering field, but another part of me is kind of like thinking, "You'll be okay." Like I have the rest of my life to kind of like work and move on up, so those are kind of like two battling things in my head. And I'd say just in general like . . . one not being – I guess like a general fear is having failure after college and not reaching my expectations of being able to be financially stable or move out. I'd say that's a worry of mine.

Jessica noted concerns about obtaining internships that were related to her intended field of work. She pointed out lukewarm feedback from companies about internship opportunities, with COVID-related communication disruptions putting a damper on plans to obtain critical apprenticeship experiences.

> I would definitely say that the top risk is definitely the communication aspect. Like I've been in communication with a few companies on just stuff like apprenticeship roles/internships or just hope they can give me a little more sort of real-world experience in the field that I want to go in and it's a little bit difficult because some of these places are sort of far out, but I'm kind of thinking with COVID it might be beneficial for me because then maybe I can do it online, but it's kind of a little up in the air because people are still, like, we're not really sure necessarily where they're going to house these programs if they're going to be . . .

In describing her work plans, Eliana, a Latina female sophomore at a four-year private college who played tennis and worked part time as a tutor, hoped to stay in the U.S. after completing her degree. Despite conveying a very positive attitude about her undergraduate experience, she shared worries about the pursuit of post-college job opportunities. She described the challenge of adapting to the realities of xenophobic attitudes in the U.S., discerning how to navigate the labor market as she pursued her planned career after she graduates, while finding a work environment where she could be welcomed:

> Okay, well, I feel like sometimes there is some xenophobia towards Latinos, which makes me a little scared when I start working. So I know that it will be difficult for people who are used to living with people, for example, who only speak English, then suddenly a person who speaks another language will arrive and say, well, maybe this person will not be able to explain himself/herself the same or maybe this person will not be able to understand me as an American person would understand me, let's put it like this. Therefore, I feel that the matter of language, of culture is complicated, because it may be very easy for me to arrive at a place and feel very comfortable but for other people it may not be.

Eliana also shared:

> I am conscious that it is culturally very difficult, let´s say, for the people from certain areas as well as the ones that aren´t from such areas to receive new people because it is always like—for the ones that are used to working with something and with certain people, changes will always be difficult, so I believe it is very important for me to be able to manage that but also that for me to know how to manage that.

Crystal also expressed readying herself for challenges associated with being an African American woman in the tech field and thinking about how to orient to the headwinds she would find:

> [S]o we know the STEM field is not diverse, so it's particularly heterosexual, White men. So I'm going into that as an African American woman in CS [computer science] where our numbers are very small I'm just worried that the things I'll say just won't be, like, acknowledged or taken seriously, or I'll just kind of be like I'll say something but it'll be kind of disregarded and they just go about their day because they're not, you know, it's not diverse amount exposed to a multitude of just different individuals, not just Black women ourselves, but other POC [people of color]. And it's changing, I'm acknowledging that, so, yeah, it's getting better, but it's not where we need to be currently.
>
> So that is probably my biggest worry; just feeling like if I get shut down, like if they say something I just shut down, like I'm not going to go against it is another thing I'm going to have to work on, and I feel like that's also going to be another challenge. Whether that be like people I'm working with on a project or, like, my coworkers.

Crystal also conveyed how she could build a supportive network in her career and her expectations for supports that might be provided by her prospective employers:

> So if they have a diversity inclusion group, I'm pretty sure [tech] companies do have that, definitely being part of that. Becoming friends with – not trying to say, like, becoming friends with the POC – the company, but just having strong connections, like, ties with them. So like when I go through something, like, okay, here's another person who knows what I'm going through. Although that's not to say that a Caucasian person will not understand what I'm going through, they can, but I don't feel like it's going to be on the same level as a person of color.

Holly talked about tensions regarding her choice to move away from home to pursue her ambitions to work at a large company, and how her intentions elicit disparate reactions from family members and family friends:

> I think the first thing [regarding work challenges] would probably be the culture shock of, like, being away from my parents because that's a huge deal for a girl in a Middle Eastern family to move out before she's married and all that. It's a huge thing so I probably would get like a lot of backlash for it from my family and family friends . . . [my parents] are 100 percent supportive of me even leaving for it . . . My parents are very much modernized.

Daphne highlighted the danger of burnout when framing the risks and challenges to achieving her work goals after obtaining a degree. As a student experiencing the time constraints of balancing both work and school, Daphne shared that low pay and difficulty obtaining employment during a global pandemic as potentially enduring challenges:

> One I guess would be the conditions that are, again, unequal in America, you know, whether that be minimum wage not being enough to kind of like give people what they need to have a quality life, or just, you know, opportunities like we're in a pandemic and, you know, things are very limited. It's hard to get out there. I feel like that's definitely a challenge when trying to find work. I guess also time is an issue, as well. And they kind of go hand-in-hand because I feel like the more you work, the more you get paid, but then it's like is it really equaling out; you know what I'm saying? Like I'm studying like 40 hours, working and it's not enough and then that time isn't being made for other things, not even just education but, like, you know, time for joy or just free time, you know, just that burnout. I feel like that's very common with any type of job even if I did have a degree.

Respondents who worked provided interesting insights on the motivations for pursuing their work efforts while enrolled in college. The nature of the work varied, where there was both full-time, part-time employment, and one-demand ("gig") work arrangements that included language tutors, freelance transcriber, soccer coach, and online shop owner (see Chapter 3 for a summary of participant occupations).

Sources of Support

As young adults navigate risks and challenges related to the shock of COVID-19, they can be aided by the presence of supports that can serve a protective function, permitting cultivation of commensurate coping processes. The exploration of these sources of support in the interview was motivated by the following interview protocol questions:

Supports can be persons, agencies, organizations, or other entities that help you meet your needs and navigate challenges. What kinds of supports help you cope with challenges or risks you are facing at school? At work?
How long does it take for you to access the most important supports to you?

When asked about sources of supports, the primary themes across all resource levels were friends or members of peer groups, families, academic advisors or professors, or affinity groups. Those participants who were working also referenced co-workers as sources of support. Students also spoke about the need to take care of their mental health as they managed stress and anxiety, echoing participants' references to mental health in participants' response to questions regarding changes to education plans and goals. In terms of accessibility to supports, the time to reach a support ranged from less than an hour to a day. Only one participant, who relied upon supports at their school, reported having to endure a two-week wait for support.

Among participants who referenced family as a significant source of support, familial expectations were embedded in cultural norms, particularly those whose families immigrated to the U.S., and informed their view of participants educational paths.

Cheryl was a first year Biochemistry major at a four-year private university who was taking courses in person at her university's campus at the time of her interview. She relayed receiving considerable emotional support from her family, particularly her parents, when she was feeling down and the coping with pressure of her studies:

> Cause like I know specifically emotionally wise, or when I'm just feeling down and like everything is just like – every assignment is there, I like seek

> support from my friends and my family and like specifically my parents and just call them up and like, "Oh, this is happening to me, like, oh my gosh." And they're like always there to be like, "It's okay, it's okay, you got this. We know you're amazing, you will do great. Like we're here if you need anything." And it's just like me ranting or like me hearing them, I don't know, brightens my day and just reminds me it's okay, and just like to say things like, "Don't take things too hard."

Of consideration for some individuals is their connectivity to family and achieving a balance between their familial obligations and the exploration afforded by a postsecondary education to define and attain their personal goals. In Alan's case, his older brother's experience familiarizing their parents with a career path that was considered unconventional made it easier for Alan to explore novel interests with more freedom in order to choose a field that interested him:

> I also have an older brother and he's about eight years older than me and we went through the struggle, too, because he originally, he is also a computer science major and now he's like working at a tech company and all that. And I feel like my brother and I—we're very stubborn; like we did not let our parents influence our career choices. And so he had to fight his way to prove that, you know, computer science is like an actual pathway here. But that's like not even imaginable in Vietnam and so it took them, oh, like, "You can get paid for this?" And they can actually see what he's making and now they're more like, they're completely fine with it, but during college they were definitely, like, "Oh, why don't you try medical?" You know, like, in the medical field. And, yeah, eventually I think he has sort of made the path easier for me and so when I got to school my parents just let me choose whatever I wanted.

School-based resources and supports helped students cope with COVID-19 learning and living conditions. From connecting with mentors to participating in support groups and workshops, Crystal referenced the fact that her university had more mentors and supports than she could count, allowing her to feel fully supported in navigating her first year of college remotely. Cheryl also took advantage of student wellness resources at her university to help her manage stress:

> [I]ndividual like one-on-one therapy is what I'm currently at. And then also just taking advantage of the gym and like you know, helping myself, I guess like finding a way to destress in times like to [sic] school and everything, and I found it very fun. And like now that it's getting hot outside, I'll probably take walks again like I did in the fall, so I'm very excited.

Alternatively, Daphne relayed how seeking care for mental health struggles was complicated by the lack of timely access to care, exacerbated by services moving to virtual contexts. She had trouble accessing timely support at both school and work, sharing:

> I receive accommodations because I struggle with mental health for school; however there are times where, like, I need to reach out to somebody and I don't hear a response back at all and that might be due to, like, the fact that we're in a virtual world, things are harder to keep up with; or just like, I don't know, what we're talking about earlier which is people advocating that they're there for you, but never actualizing it. So usually it's like a week or longer than a few weeks or, again, sometimes not at all.

In describing the supports offered by her employer, she stated:

> They're flawed . . . I feel like it's kind of like a front, like—okay, they'll advertise the themselves as like 'We're here for you,' but then when I voice a need they're like, 'Eh, nothing we can really do, you're just another employee.'

Daphne was the only participant who communicated that her employers offered access to supportive resources. It is unclear if the lack of responsiveness was owed to technical issues or another reason, but it is clear that she experienced disappointment when she was not able to access the offered supports.

James attends college in the U.S., far from his family, who lives in a country in Sub-Saharan Africa. He provided novel insights on the efficacy of distal and proximal supports in place prior to the onset of the pandemic, expressing deep appreciation of his college's generosity as he navigated coming to attend school in the U.S. with few resources. He was imbued with a positive outlook and drive to do well, bolstered by encouragement from his family, particularly his grandmother, to remain positive.

> I'm here [in the U.S.] pretty much solo. My mom lives in [country name] and she can't help . . . So that [college tuition] is a really big challenge for my family. But I don't blame anyone of that. It's just the condition that they are in.
>
> Because nobody in my family has been to college, so I just went on online video platform and watched a couple of videos of what it looks like in college, and all the kids on those videos, they have a lot of stuff in their room, and all the stuff that they—I used to live in New Jersey, and so I was travelling away from New Jersey with just my travel backpack, a few clothes, and I was just worried that—how would I make it through college? How would I get money to buy books and everything, and then—but then I resumed college. I found out

> that the school already set up everything for me. In my room, they already put me a microwave, TV, fridge, essentials for reading, books, and like way, way beyond everything I needed. Like, way beyond, the school supplied what I needed. I haven't even opened some of them, so the school has been really, really tremendous in that aspect.

The sense of support James felt from his school was deeply felt and appreciated. He continued:

> It [the assistance from his institution] made me feel appreciative, to be honest. I felt really emotional. If you can tell, I still feel emotional the way I'm saying it right now, because I never had anything easy in life. So that just showed that like, a couple of people appreciate you and a couple of people care about your wellbeing and that they just want to see you succeed without wanting anything back from you. That's really, really great.

". . . it's not high school anymore. You gotta do it, now you're an adult now." – Jessica, 1st Year Computer Science major.

James' experiences as a first-generation student highlight the critical role that active supports can play in a positive postsecondary experience, buffering reverberations of shocks. When asked about the role of supports, Crystal, also a first-generation college student, shared:

> Yes. I know who they [supports] are, but, like, I think I have – I don't even know, like first of all, so many advisors, I'm like that is so perfect . . . So I'm never confused about, "Well, what classes should I take?" Or, "I need help finding this." Or, "I don't know what to do." Cause, like, I know who my advisors are and I know how to get to all of them, and they're pretty responsive, as well.

Crystal accessed the institution-wide support group for underrepresented students, which also offered workshops to provide students' additional supports (e.g., financial literacy). Her participation in an affinity-based group focused on African American students provided tremendous resources and was well supported with its own tutors. These first generation and affinity-based supports were augmented by the university-wide academic services. She considered herself very well supported by her institution but did note that students must take the initiative to access them:

> So the campus is amazing with resources and just helping students; you just have to really take initiative and find them or else you're just going to kind of be like lost, you know? And they're not going to reach out to you.

The overwhelming sentiment was positive for students who understood and were able to take advantage of institutional supports and resources during COVID-19.

Spatial Characteristics and Developmental Contexts

COVID-19 public health restrictions resulted in the closure or limited physical, general public access to buildings and structures. As such, an in-person assessment of the utility of assets was not feasible for the study. Further, assumptions regarding the nature and character of the person-context dynamic that presupposes individuals' physical navigation of geographic areas were rendered obsolete as remaining safe from infection was a primary imperative shaping personal and social safety decisions. Nonetheless, it was still possible to capture information on the characteristics of participants' lived environments to gain insights on the attributes of their developmental contexts. School closures and the movement to life online severely curtailed the ability to move freely to carry out daily activities. Further, this also translated to the nature of the conduct of the interviews themselves, as the study transitioned to interviews utilizing an online conferencing tool. Even with the dominance of online tools for carrying out previous in-person activities for those with stable internet access and sufficiently resourced (e.g., attending school, shopping, telehealth), life was still lived in physical spaces. It is useful, then, to ascertain where participants were situated relative to key assets that allowed them to carry out key functions and meet their needs. To obtain this information, the interview protocol asked participants to provide the zip codes where they resided, attended school and worked to better understand their developmental contexts during COVID-19. The geographical distance between residential and school zip codes are found in Table 5.3. Study participants hailed from diverse geographic regions in the U.S., residing in states located on the West Coast, the Midwest, the Midsouth, and the Northeast. Table 5.3 also provides a summary of the distance data with breakouts by institutional type, where provided.

Table 5.3 Distance between Residence and School (n = 18)

	Average Distance between Residence and School (miles)	*Distance Range Between Residence and School (miles)*
All Study Participants (n = 18)	199.7	0–990
Participants Enrolled in Two-Year Postsecondary Institution (n = 3)*	4	2–6
Participants Enrolled in Four-Year Postsecondary Institution (n = 14)*	250.8	0–990

**Note:* One respondent did not specify institution type as such the total participant count by the two institution types is 17.

Table 5.4 Participant Assets—One-Mile Radius

Zip Code	*Parks*	*Shopping*	*Hospital/ Medical Center*	*Community College/University*	*Gym/Recreation Center*
1	X	X			X
2	X	X			X
3	X			X	
4	X	X			
5	X	X		X	X
6	X	X	X		
7	X	X		X	X
8		X	X		
9*	X	X	X		X
10	X	X	X		X
11	X	X		X	X
12	X	X	X	X	X
13	X	X		X	X
14	X	X	X	X	X

Note: Four study participants resided in one zip code (noted in the table with "*"), hence the total number of zip codes adds up to 14; While Gym/Recreational facilities can exist within university or community college campuses, for the purposes of this analysis these assets refer to those listed as accessible to the public either as part of a public park system or through private fee-based membership.

In general, respondents who attended two-year institutions lived in locations close to their institutions, while the majority (11) of those attending four-year institutions resided further from home, with six of the 14 participants attending schools that were over 75 miles from their stated residence, and five of the six enrolled at an institution over 100 miles from their residence. Only two of the nine participants who worked did so at a non-school and non-residential location. The remainder either worked on campus (n = 5) or from home (n = 2).

The study captured basic information on the assets, or those organizations or entities that provide support or aided in meeting basic needs or deliver essential supports. Utilizing the zip codes provided by participants regarding where they lived at the time of the interview, an online mapping tool identified assets that were located within a one-mile radius of the study participants' location. Table 5.4 presents a summary of key asset categories.

Additionally, it is important to note that no student participants identified experiencing food insecurity or housing instability, nor was there any reference to challenges accessing technology or transportation resources for meeting daily needs. The absence of any mention of these challenges does not imply that these adversities were not present at the time of the interview, but they were not highlighted or referenced as experienced risks or challenges.

The internet served as a developmental context during the period of time in which the qualitative interviews were conducted. Certainly, cultivation of resilience and coping strategies is borne of navigating challenges that, in turn, surface in-depth knowledge of self, especially when enhanced by the presence of active and engaged supports. For the students in the qualitative component, email, texting, and web-enabled conferencing tools were critical to remaining in communication with supportive people in their network during the COVID-19 public health restrictions. As such, it raises the importance of web-based communication tools and social media during shocks facilitating and mediating access to supports during shocks. Specifically, the significance of online information sharing and social engagement that framed developmental contexts during the COVID-19 pandemic must be acknowledged. The recessionary and public health shock phenomena had global and local repercussions that reorganized how to understand the interrelated nature of distal (e.g., global, national) and proximal (e.g., local community, educational setting, home) contexts. This was particularly noteworthy in considering interconnected, immediate communication channels, especially social media. Government agencies and policy makers, at the forefront of making decisions and shaping protocols that would govern how countries would face and recover from shocks, were at the crossroads of the race between fact and fiction. Just over a decade after the end of the Great Recession, when the COVID-19 pandemic arrived, the acceleration of information sharing through social media increased exponentially, further rearranging assumptions regarding how individuals remained connected and became informed about how best to navigate the shock.

In sum, the global pandemic effectively forced broad scale addoption of internet-based tools at school and work for those resourced and with internet access. In this period of public health restrictions and social isolation to stop the spread of the virus, virtual tools on the internet stepped into the void created by the closure of schools and work places, becoming developmental domains unto themselves, supplanting other gathering places where social ties could be reinforced (e.g., churches, community centers, entertainment venues). (It is important to note that frontline workers in health, safety, and food service in particular remained at risk of exposure as their professions required in person presence.) For those who were living and working in virtual spaces only, it created an almost claustrophobic sensation in an altered reality as in-person contact with people outside of trusted "pods" would entail risk and necessitate protective protocols to avoid possible infection. Alternatiely, many could find new paths for building community based on shared experiences and interests not found in their immediate lived environment (as with non-internet contexts, these connections varied in their quality, safety, and capacity to support positive identity development). During this period, a reliable prediction or forecast for when these specters of infection and restrictions might recede remained elusive, further complicated by soaring misinformation undermining scientific, evidence-based information on how to remain safe. The developmental implications of enrolled young adults living life online are are noted by the findings in this study and will be a subject of study for years to come.

A Life Course Understanding of Identity Development

> It's been difficult since graduating from high school and kind of just like being exposed to this whole new world of adulthood. It kind of feels like, you know, you got this new video game but nobody gave you an instruction manual, so you're just kind of out here figuring it out. And that might be the case for even 20 to 25-year-olds, you know, but I also feel like a lot of the things that we struggle with in terms of like work and school can be prevented if like there were just bigger changes in certain systems.
>
> –David

Across the quantitative and qualitative components, the findings presented here identify patterns of sustained postsecondary enrollment and adaptations as the Great Recession and the COVID-19 global shocks were underway. The quantitative findings drawn from the PSID-TA reveal sustained engagement with postsecondary enrollment for cross-sectional cohorts of 18- to 20-year-olds under study. Further, the ways in which the Great Recession altered education plans for participants enrolled in postsecondary education varied. The qualitative component's phenomenological interview approach permitted deep exploration of diverse young adult meaning making and feelings about navigating the COVID-19 shock and the disruption accompanying a period already rife with change acclimating to the first or second year of postsecondary enrollment. Indeed, navigating the reverberations of asymmetric shocks can be fraught with confusion, with no handbook or instruction manual available to explain how to approach quotidian activities, let alone the pursuit of a milestone like postsecondary degree attainment. To be clear, life is full of challenges and unanticipated disruptions that can provide opportunities for building new skills and approaches not considered under typical conditions.

The enrolled students coping and living through the COVID-19 shock in particular is a unique young adult group, having experienced two shocks before the age of 25, as both adolescents (the Great Recession) and young adults (COVID-19 pandemic). The other unique aspect of this young adult cohort is the incorporation, as a result of the pandemic, of the internet as a developmental context.

A Disruptive Period Encounters Shock

The priority for this study was to capture, within a person-context theoretical framing, how diverse young adults during shock periods of identity transition after high school were developing their identity in service to broader personal and professional aspirations. For those enrolled in postsecondary education, students are primed to be in a state of exploration of different pathways available to them in keeping with a young adult life stage rife with transitions and novel experiences. Post high school graduation, then, identities are in state of readiness for "what comes next." This can be experienced with excitement, trepidation, or both, accompanied by a sense of vulnerability about not exactly knowing what awaits them on their journeys to adulthood. It may be that being primed for change provides a suppleness of identity that enhances these diverse young adults' capacity to adapt in the moment to unanticipated changes. Viewed, then, as a developmental task, postsecondary education advances identity journeys. These journeys can involve risks and challenges, and the implications of these phenomena are shaped by the presence of and accessibility to resources and supports in developmental contexts. In effect, in the midst of seismic shifts, a shock, while disruptive, occurs in the midst of other significant disruptions associated with transitions in students' lives and educational contexts. As such, that a shock occurred during this already disruptive period for these enrolled young adults may have facilitated an absorption of the shocks' effects in a way not possible for persons at other life stages where identity-linked endeavors have more established patterns, practices, and protocols for individuals to know they are on track. Certainly, the participants interviewed had attained the milestone of securing enrollment in a postsecondary institution. As such, even though the institutions where participants were enrolled were struggling to varying degrees with transitions to online learning, and students struggled with the challenges and distractions of the altered learning environments, overall participants conveyed a sense of self-efficacy in navigating their educational and work obligations. There was a willingness to make alterations in their education plans, thus sustaining the identity-building task in tact in the midst of a shock.

The diverse young adults under study were at a critical developmental stage between adolescence and adulthood, with related experiences affirmative of the complexity, uncertainty, and optimism of negotiating novel experiences associating with burgeoning adult identities that collided with the dynamic shock reverberations.

Next, Chapter 6 reflects on these findings and discusses considerations for advancing a novel theoretical perspective on the person-context dimensions of human development during shock conditions. The Dynamic Ecological Systems Theory of Identity Development (DESTID) is informed by experiences of diverse young adults navigating new avenues of identity development when their contexts were disrupted and rearranged. In particular, the pursuit of higher education provided a purpose that helped sustain identity building properties. Interviews conducted during COVID-19 also reveal a process among many of re-evaluating which among the varied courses of study responded to a changing set of interests, needs and aspirations. Within DESTID, we observe, then, a process of emergence, whereby shock conditions bring about a discernment regarding the nature and type of educational pursuits undertaken. Participants, while remaining steadfast in their commitment to pursuing their postsecondary education, either affirm or call into question the course of study they had planned. While the exploratory function of this period of life presumes a re-evaluation, culling, and re-selection of pathways, the interviews established that this process is anchored to the COVID-19 shock in particular. In the case of PSID and the Great Recession, the "Changing of major" further establishes the emergence link, whereby the alteration of the course of study is what emerges as a common action taken in response to the shock.

References

Bennett, J., & Kochhar, R. (2019). Two recessions, two recoveries. *Pew Research Center*. https://www.pewresearch.org/social-trends/2019/12/13/two-recessions-two-recoveries/

Centers for Disease Control. (2020). Temporary halt in residential evictions to prevent the further spread of COVID-19. *Federal Register, National Archives and Records Administration*. Retrieved from https://www.federalregister.gov/documents/2020/09/04/2020-19654/temporary-halt-in-residential-evictions-to-prevent-the-further-spread-of-covid-19.

Farber, H. S. (2015). Job loss in the Great Recession and its aftermath: US evidence from the displaced workers survey (No. w21216). National Bureau of Economic Research.

García-Morales, V. J., Garrido-Moreno, A., & Martín-Rojas, R. (2021). The transformation of higher education after the COVID disruption: Emerging challenges in an online learning scenario. *Frontiers in psychology*, *12*, 616059.

Panel Study of Income Dynamics, public use dataset. (2017). Survey Research Center, Institute for Social Research, University of Michigan, Ann Arbor, MI

Passmore, W., & Sherlund, S. M. (2016). Government-Backed Mortgage Insurance, Financial Crisis, and the Recovery from the Great Recession. Federal Reserve Board.

Weinberg, J. (2013). The Great Recession and its aftermath. Federal Reserve History, 3.

6 Dynamic Ecological Systems Theory of Identity Development—A New Paradigm of Shock—Informed Young Adult Identity Development Research

> [I]n high school, you know, like I feel like I didn't receive proper guidance and kind of like a smooth transition into this whole new world and there were also just like, you know, inequalities there like, you know, sometimes not having like an access to better education because of where you come from. Like in your neighborhood, like there's so many things that we struggle with, not even just this bracket of like 18 to 20, but I'm sure, you know, older adults with children and stuff like that, like this is either the time we're living in, or this is just years of things that need to be restored . . . so, I don't know, I'm hoping that like the more people gain understanding of just, like, what's happening and what's being struggled with, the more we can just like help to address that, I guess.
>
> Daphne, first year community college student

Swimming with the Current and Encountering Gale Force Winds

Daphne portrayed an awareness of the cross currents encountered when navigating postsecondary transitions, and the life course implications of coping with systemic shocks. For those young adults transitioning to postsecondary education pathways specifically, the guidance, support, resources, and lessons learned to build a sense of self-efficacy were under review and revision to meet the obligations, challenges, and opportunities they encounter. The 18- to 20-year-old cohorts studied here were engaged in developmental tasks, i.e., education, in contexts (school, work, home) under duress during shock periods. These asymmetric events made it clear that navigating a new ocean of possibilities after high school would not follow normative patterns: where diverse young adults had to learn to marshal new and pre-existing resources to cope with gale force winds waging during shocks. Findings presented here show that for enrolled young adults, sustained engagement in their education provided an ameliorative stabilizing property, aided by accessing supports to engage novel risks during a dynamic period of heightened risk. Indeed, the robust finding from the national panel survey and qualitative interviews shows that racially and ethnically diverse young adults from different regions of the U.S. exhibit adaptive coping and creativity in the midst of extreme societal disruption.

DOI: 10.4324/9781003404842-6

The person-context pillar set forth in EST and PVEST hold in this study, where it is clear that these shocks altered developmental contexts in which individuals, here young adults, carried out development enhancing tasks. The Dynamic Ecological Systems Theory of Identity builds on these theories' insights to ascertain how disruptions in developmental contexts affect identity development paths presumed to follow normative paths in the relatively stable domains of postsecondary education. These shocks, particularly the COVID-19 pandemic, marked the arrival of dynamic uncertainty to the presumed stable developmental contexts: Participants faced society-wide shocks that had system-level reverberations, impacting both proximal and distal domains. With COVID-19, the impacts of the public health emergency rearranged both the location and function of activities that resided in each of the nested systems conceptualized by Bronfenbrenner's EST, rendering the distinction between home and school, work and home, diffused if not erased altogether. For example, one of the qualitative interview participants (Ana) was living at home, where she both attended courses and ran an online business. Another (Robert) held an online remote position as a closed captionist that he could carry out on-demand, setting his hours. Indeed, half of the participants worked in positions while they were enrolled. The dynamic, overlapping domains where students engaged in school and work obliations were no longer discrete and the capacity of institutions in particular to provide supportive resources varied. As such, when considering identity development during shock periods, a shock-sensitive theoretical approach emerges in order to permit considering the interactive dynamics of context and identity during shocks. Further, it is necessary to identify the stabilizing effects offered by identity-building pursuits. The next section details how such a novel theoretical approach is supported by insights garnered from the mixed-methods study of diverse young adults during the Great Recession and the COVID-19 global pandemic.

Exogenous Shocks and Young Adulthood

This mixed-methods study set out to examine how an exogenous shock shifts underlying assumptions about the achievement of postsecondary education as an integral milestone in the young adulthood developmental period and identity development specifically. Utilizing an Adapted Explanatory Sequential Design, the research questions guiding this study were as follows:

- How were the postsecondary education and working patterns for low-income, high-achieving young adults shaped by the Great Recession in comparison to their high-income counterparts?
- How did the Great Recession impact education planning for young adults between the ages of 18 and 20, the key age range for college going?
- Eleven years after the Great Recession ended, have there been any changes in the key factors that inform education planning for young adults between the ages of 18 and 20?

The findings of each study component are discussed in the following and then brought into conversation to advance novel insights on identity development for diverse young adult populations during shock periods.

Quantitative Component Findings

In the PSID-TA module, the postsecondary enrollment trend line before (i.e., 2005 and 2007 data cohorts), during (i.e., 2009 and 2011 data cohorts), and after (i.e., 2013 cohort) the Great Recession echoes patterns observed in U.S. Federal data presented in Chapter 1. The quantitative study prioritized examining the enrollment experiences of below-median-income young adults, with comparisons to their above-median-income counterparts to illuminate differences based on income-based resource levels. Here, an overall increase in postsecondary enrollment for young adults between 18 and 20 years old occurred that decreased by 2013 after the Great Recession was declared over, even though as its most acute effects receded for many, recovery did not restore what had been lost, particularly African Americans. Overall, below-median-income young adults enrolled in postsecondary education at a lower rate than their above-median-income young adults. In terms of the Great Recession changing education plans, while the descriptive findings showed a greater proportion of below-median-income young adults changing plans than higher resourced young adults, a statistically significant difference is only observed in 2011, indicating the economic shock's impact on the education planning of below-median-income students was short-lived.

Education Plans Under Revision. For respondents who reported they would change education plans, changing one's major was a top choice. Interestingly, none of the 2009, 2011, and 2013 Great Recession cohorts reported dropping out of school or postponing education as changes they would pursue, indicating that among the response options available none included suspending postsecondary education pursuits. This finding not only aligns with the overall increase in enrollment reported earlier but also conveys the durability of commitment to staying the course in remaining enrolled when the Great Recession was in full force. It's important to note that this durability may have been facilitated by an increase in student loan debt (United States Government Accountability Office, 2022) that would endure for years to come. The education planning of young adults who were working but not enrolled was also studied to explore the impacts for young adults whose pathways did not include postsecondary education at the time of the interviews. Here, among PSID-TA (PSID, 2021) sample members in this category who were classified below-median-income young adults, the Great Recession had no impact on their education planning across the three cohorts that reported on this question; only one above-median-income, working, non-enrolled young adult stated that the Great Recession altered their education plans.

Elaborating Income Categories for PSID-TA Enrolled Respondents. A review of the sample as it is broken down into low, middle, and high-income categories helps provide a more nuanced understanding of how the PSID-TA

Table 6.1 Enrollment by Low, Middle, and High Income

Year	*Low Income*	*Middle Income*	*High Income*
2005 Income Range (n)	0–$30,404 (71)	$30,416–$70,536 (94)	$70,737–$1,460,000 (173)
2007 Income Range (n)	0–$34,900 (56)	$35,000–$75,350 (93)	$77,000–$2,133,500 (168)
2009 Income Range (n)	0–$35,413 (55)	$35,456–$78,848 (92)	$78,867–$2,067,000 (180)
2011 Income Range (n)	0–$30,404 (51)	$30,416–$70,536 (131)	$79,737–$1,460,000 (179)
2013 Income Range (n)	0–$31,722 (48)	$31,838–$72,276 (91)	$72,420–$3,222,000 (175)

Source: Panel Study of Income Dynamics, public use dataset, 2021

sample members are arrayed across high, medium, and low-income categories. Table 6.1 presents the descriptive summaries of these income groups, including the ranges for these categories for all enrolled young adults, and the number of 18- to 20-year-olds who were enrolled in college in the given year who fell into a particular income group. While these grouping proportions are not to be directly compared to those of the qualitative component participants, it does provide a clearer picture of how survey respondents are situated across more refined income categories. Of particular note is that most enrolled students fell into the high-income category, which, given the presence of greater financial resources than their low- and middle-income counterparts, may be a driver behind the finding that above-median-income respondents' weathered the effects of the Great Recession more effectively. In effect, these counts show that students from high-income categories remained enrolled in numbers greater than their low- and middle-income counterparts, in alignment with the descriptive findings for the above-median-income group in Chapter 4. This result is also confirmatory of findings from Nau (2016) and Cozzolino, Smith, and Crosnoe (2018), which revealed that higher income families weathered the Great Recession more effectively.

Qualitative Component Findings

In the Adapted Explanatory Sequential Design undertaken for the study, the quantitative data results framed the content and approach for the qualitative component. Through the phenomenological interviews, it was possible to explore themes and concepts raised by respondents, eliciting richer, emergent data regarding young adult education and work goals in the U.S. during a period of a global, exogenous shock.

The qualitative study involved 18 phenomenological interviews with racially and ethnically diverse 18- to 20-year-olds from varied geographic areas in the U.S., enrolled in both four-year and two-year postsecondary institutions. Given that the interviews were conducted during the COVID-19 global pandemic, study participants were attending school either virtually or in a hybrid arrangement. The vast majority of participants stated that the public health emergency and the economic recession precipitated by the economic slowdown did not alter their education plans. For those who noted that their education plans changed, they primarily cited changes in their major or altering their course enrollment. One person noted he was thinking more seriously about pursuing his true interests in a way he had not before; another talked about the practicalities of a day job while accommodating his true love of astronomy. All interview participants conveyed a commitment to achieving their planned education and work goals but many did note the difficulties negotiating the day-to-day challenges of online education and life during COVID-19.

The qualitative interviews reveal real-time experiences of participants as they were actively making meaning of their struggles, challenges, and risks to meet their obligations as students under incredibly difficult circumstances. Further, half of the participants held part-time, full-time, or on-demand ("gig") employment, collapsing the discrete student/worker categories utilized for the quantitative analyses. As a result, the data reveal the experiences of diverse young adults who were handling the proximate struggles associated with managing multiple roles as students and workers: meeting the demands of rigorous undergraduate programs of study while managing job responsibilities. For many, challenges and risks to their education and work goals centered on the online, remote nature of online education, with concerns about finances and mental health prominent themes that came through in the data. Additional concerns were related to obtaining internships while enrolled and an awareness that racial and ethnic inequality and tensions could negatively impact professional pathways. No person stated an inability to meet their daily needs, with the vast majority of participants designating themselves as "medium resourced," conveying an overall material security. It is important to note that participants were primarily located either at their homes with their families or in their dormitories on their campuses at the time of the interviews; as such, the presence of familial and institutional supports played a significant role in their assessment of their resource status. This is important, as during this time the U.S. government issued grants to postsecondary institutions, including funds granted directly to enrolled students, delivered financial support to families, and implemented eviction protections. This had the salutary effect of stabilizing critical resources needed for meeting daily needs at the population level. This large-scale deployment of resources was unique in the U.S. and aligns with findings regarding the positive effects of institutional supports during COVID-19 in countries outside the U.S. (Plakhotnik, Volkova, Jiang, Yahiaoui, Pheiffer, McKay, Newman, & Reißig-Thust, 2021). Participants also demonstrated adaptive coping strategies in how they engaged challenges and risks, relying on the supportive families, friends, and resources at their postsecondary institutions (e.g., mentoring supports for first-generation students, academic advisors, helpful professors) that aided their sustained engagement with the education and work goals they established prior to the onset of the pandemic.

Young Adulthood under Construction

Elder acknowledges the simultaneity of life roles as an under-interrogated phenomenon in life course theory that was not considered in the initial edition of *Children of the Great Depression*. Certainly, the data from the qualitative interviews demonstrate that the balancing of multiple roles was ever present among these study participants. Specifically, while the study engaged their postsecondary education experiences and pathways as the domain of primary research interest vis-à-vis identity development, the multiple facets of the participants' lives were discussed in the assessment of risk, challenges, and supports. Nearly all participants referenced roles, relationships, and connections to endeavors that they inhabited and balanced in their daily lives. In addition to their status as students, participants were freelance workers, interns, sons, daughters, grandchildren, siblings, nieces, nephews, grandchildren, community members, first-generation college students, and mentors. All of these carried unique responsibilities, privileges, obligations, challenges, and rewards, both immediate and deferred, that filled in components of a burgeoning sense of self promised by enrollment in postsedondary education. Some of these roles and responsibilities resided in disparate domains, for example, Daphne who had an ambition to be an adolescent behavioral therapist and worked 40 hours a week as a cashier, or Ana who built a successful online business, which was not related to her studies. Generally, participants' responses conveyed a tenacity in managing the overlapping and interrelated realms of activity underway at the time of the interviews.

In sum, all young adults communicated thoughtfulness and commitment to their education and work goals in spite of their struggles with navigating altered postsecondary education contexts. Students did not express problems with the technology utilized for online courses, work obligations, or engaging with friends. Despite the ease of use with the mechanics of new learning tools, many seemed to adapt as best they could as their institutions adjusted to the realities of teaching and mentoring under public health restrictions, while other participants shared struggles with connecting with teachers and fellow students. As they managed distractions of an online learning environment and struggled in some cases to forge social connections with their peers, it appeared that most participants found stability in keeping to the routine that their course-taking obligations, along with work responsibilities, permitted. The economic toll of the pandemic-related recession did not bring about additional changes to their postsecondary plans, as many participants highlighted the durability of the financial support they received through scholarship programs or the provision of resources from schools. However, others raised financial concerns when asked about the risks and challenges they encountered, not linked to the pandemic-induced recession per se. Overall, the findings point to a clear commitment on the part of these young adults to make sense of their pursuits in the face of profound constraints and restrictions that were imposed as a result of the global pandemic and recession. While their education journeys may not have represented the caliber of academic work and engagement they hoped for, remaining connected to the objectives they set for themselves prior to the onset of the pandemic may have provided critical stability during a period of extreme uncertainty and risk.

It is interesting to note that when asked about resources and supports, no participant referenced assets situated in locations near their residences (e.g., parks, social services, stores). This may have been owed to COVID-19 closures. Indeed, the data suggest a reliance upon online tools to meet needs, with no reference to accessing resources in-person. As such, the concept of geographically specified spatial inequality in lived environments did not align with the COVID-19-closure reality of young adults' lived environments. Indeed, it is important to incorporate the virtual dimensions of developmental contexts, given exclusive reference to home-based (i.e., family), online, or phone/text-based access to supports. Broadly, this finding would point to the importance of accounting for unequal access to the internet, or the digital divide, where risks, challenges, resources, and supports exist and can be engaged to varying degrees based on where a person is located in a given area (U.S. General Accountability Office, 2022, 2023) (e.g., under-resourced rural and urban areas where broadband access follows broader patterns of inequality).

Overall Findings from Quantitative and Qualitative Components: A Dynamic Ecological Systems Theory of Identity Development Emerges

The key shared finding across the quantitative and qualitative components was that enrolled young adults remained committed to their academic trajectories in the midst of world-shaking shocks. The phenomenological interviews that pointed to changes some made in their education plans in response to the effects of the shocks revealed an adaptive coping skill set. This finding is robust across the varied income and resource support categories during both shocks. As such, it demonstrates that the dynamic, radiating effects of shocks on the broader developmental contexts that undergo epic transformations are met by enrolled young adult adaptivity, bolstered by immediate access to supports suited to the particularities of the individual lived environments (i.e., dorms, home). Persons living at home, particularly first-year students who missed out on critical connections at the start of their college career, pushed through disappointment and relied on supportive family members to make it through. Other participants who remained on campus shared the positive benefits of on-campus resources (e.g., mental health support, gyms to release stress, immediate access to mentoring supports). Whether family- or institution-based, the qualitative study affirmed that supports mattered greatly for navigating shock conditions.

Interconnected Systems, Individual Interactions. Bronfenbrenner's Ecological Systems Theory (Bronfenbrenner, 1993) depicts a series of nested systems that envelop an individual and frame their developmental journey. With

Phenomenological Variant of Ecological Systems Theory, Spencer sets forth that there are individual meaning making processes occurring in response to the presence of risks and challenges in developmental contexts. The associated presence or absence of the ameliorative character of protective factors in developmental contexts (e.g., supportive adults, organizations, racial/ethnic identity, cultural practices) informs the cultivation of coping strategies, which can be a recursive exercise as individuals advance across developmental stages across the life course. These coping strategies can be on a continuum between adaptive or maladaptive, with trial and error occurring as part of the developmental enterprise. Ultimately, an identity forms shaped by these factors, contributing to positive identity development.

PVEST holds that there is a process of ascertaining and processing risk in the moment, with adaptive or maladaptive coping informed by the supports and resources available in the moment to promote, and work against, the cultivation of a positive identity. Cultural resources linked to racial and ethnic identity or religious affiliation, for example, can provide protective factors as well in that these permit for a strengths-based stance to engage challenges and risks that accompany human existence. As such, when considering the shock effects, it becomes necessary to re-assess and re-evaluate diverse young adults' capacity to cope and draw upon those resources, supports, and protective factors that are commensurate to the level and degree of risk encountered.

Understanding the nature of the systems as populated by distinctive institutional and individual actors (e.g., person-context), this study interrogates how young adults situated in these systems pursuing a developmental milestone (postsecondary education) make meaning of their identity-enhancing goals when shocks occur. How entities, such as postsecondary institutions, embedded in developmental systems respond to shocks has implications for the person-context dynamic at the heart of a human development-centered orientation to identity. This orientation, then, shapes understanding of what constitutes effective supports to offset heightened risk and how systems ensure the provision of supports to be understood as such.

During young adults' postsecondary period, identity development is elastic and dynamic. Enrolled young adults in particular are poised to engage in a broader field of exploration, rife with new experiences as they embark on a psychosocial developmental journey. As such, the findings of this research underscore the presence of heightened dynamic processes during periods of shock that constitute a distinctive developmental experience for young adults. In this study, young adults faced unanticipated risks to their education and work trajectories. Students in the qualitative component were resourceful in seeking and utilizing varied supports that served to offset the negative effects of risks while sustaining engagement with their studies in the wake of dynamic disruptions in their learning and living environments. Furthermore, the results reveal that it is important to support young adults discernment of their learning, mental health, and financial needs during disruptive periods to ensure they are able to meet their physical and psychological health needs as they discern how to cope with the unanticipated risks emanating from disruptions. It is clear from the data that as the students made meaning of their education pursuits, they were fashioning new perspectives on how to reflect who they wanted to be and the contributions they wished to make in the future.

Protective Properties. The domain of postsecondary education engaged as an identity-building pursuit reveals the protective property of the endeavor itself in the face of disruptive asymmetric events. Put another way, the data show that as students navigated the waves of shocks, postsecondary education served as a stabilizing vehicle. This was observed in the qualitative interviews among participants who remained enrolled and engaged in their studies, demonstrating a driving purpose or goal to sustain focus during a shock. The findings also demonstrated that the adaptive-maladaptive binary construct in evaluating coping responses to risk does not always sit on opposite poles on a continuum, as suggested by PVEST, but can actually be inverted depending on the exigencies of shock circumstances. For example, under non-shock conditions, leaving college to take classes remotely might be deemed maladaptive as in-person learning among peers allows for generative intellectual and social interchange. However, under the COVID-19 shock in particular, leaving school to take classes at home was a highly adaptive safe choice given the altered nature of risk, with the secondary risk associated with adjusting to distractions being tolerable relative to the greater risk of exposure to the virus. As such, persons interviewed, particularly first-year students, were in fact navigating and making sense of the nested, inverted nature of shock-linked risk: as students embarked on new journeys as college students, the shock conditions inverted norms to accommodate novel, population-wide threats that rendered approved norms untenable. Further, the shock triggered ripple effects inwardly (e.g., struggles with mental health) and outwardly (e.g., disruption in progression to career-enhancing internships). Through it all, students made adjustments in order to sustain the fidelity of their commitment to completing their course requirements. This suggests that the stability of identity-developing pursuits is of critical importance in forging a productive path through the uncertainty of shock periods. At the individual level, then, Dynamic Ecological Systems Theory of Identity Development (DESTID) allows for consideration of the dynamic rearrangement of risk, resources, and coping linked to identity developmental processes in contexts disrupted by shocks.

The theory also engages the dynamism at the developmental context level. Specifically, the realization of systemic weaknesses linked to endemic inequality caused some participants to re-evaluate their academic and career priorities and identify mental health priorities. Additionally, the fluidity of boundaries, whereby the boundaries between home, school, and work became porous (e.g., participants who attended classes and worked while quarantining with families at home), necessitates scrutiny of how research and policy treats these domains as discrete rather than overlapping and, in some cases, blended. It is reasonable to presume that upon resumption of in-person classes, the home-school-work domains might become discrete again for many students, as they leave home-based learning environments, for example. As such, the assumption of static discrete domains can now be considered circumstantial and dynamic, and not an assumed constant.

Shock(Waves) and Young Adulthood: Toward a New Human-Centered Research Regime

This book sets the Great Recession and COVID-19 as exogenous shocks in the chronosystem. While the Great Recession was an economic-based shock, its reverberations were felt across various sectors throughout society, including employment, housing, and education. The novel, COVID-19 global pandemic was an historic public health emergency that sent shockwaves through social, cultural, and economic milieus, impacting the core function of societies around the world. The human toll of the COVID-19, and its impact on global life expectancy broadly, with U.S. life expectancy for African Americans, Hispanics, and Native American groups experiencing the biggest losses (Centers for Disease Control and Prevention, 2023), will be the subject of study for years to come.

Elder notes in *Children of the Great Depression* (Elder, Bronfenbrenner, & Clausen,1999), a foundational text for life course studies, did not factor in the effect of social movements and social change. As discussed in Chapter 1, Black Lives Matter, demonstrations for gender equality, and the fight for livable wages are a few exemplars of movements that have raised awareness and a call for action to address the negative effects of enduring racism and inequity in U.S. society. Additionally, increased research acknowledging the direct linkage to the undermining of life outcomes and opportunities empirically prove this concept, anchoring current conditions in U.S. history, from the legacy of Brown versus Board of Education (Spencer and Dowd, expected 2024; Frankenberg, Ee, Ayscue, & Orfield, 2019; Franklin, Greenberg, & Pollack, 2009) to the Plessy versus Ferguson decision (Reed, 2021; Gaynor, Kang, & Williams, 2021; Francis & Darrity, 2021). U.S. Federal Reserve's recent series "The Economy and Racism" leads the discussion calling for the field of economics and fiscal system to acknowledge and address the enduring effects of racism, as operationalized and actualized in institutional settings throughout the U.S. (Smialek, 2020).

This book posits that these shock events of profound human consequence force a re-visiting of the social scientific mission of producing knowledge for the human good, underscoring the central importance of accounting for the disruptive role of exogenous shocks on human developmental pathways. As a result, the need emerges for a novel theoretical and empirical research agenda and associated policy regimes rooted in a human development approach that prioritizes longevity and positive human developmental outcomes rather than conceptualizing human beings in terms of their utility to a particular economic system. Given the profundity of loss and inequality that has emerged in the aftermath of these shocks, interdisciplinary cross-national research studies hold promise for advancing research that ameliorates lost progress on human survival and thriving while avoiding assumptions about human beings rooted in inaccuracies, stereotypes, or worse (see American Psychological Association, American Medical Association, American Economic Association, the World Bank, and the U.S. Federal Reserve Bank as exemplars of academic institutional standard bearers acknowledging and disavowing discriminatory research and implementation science practices in their fields).

It is clear that the corrosive effects of systemic inequality and discriminatory practices based on individual and group statuses (e.g., race, ethnicity, gender identity, socioeconomic status) threaten social stability, precipitating adverse conditions that can exacerbate the negative effects of shocks at the group level, with individual identity development repercussions. As such, the DESTID serves as an inclusive, strengths-based theory that engages phenomenological meaning making of diverse young adults as critical to advancing research on positive identity development during dynamic shock periods.

Strengths-Based Approach. The population under study here, diverse young adults between the ages of 18 and 20, are unique in that in their lifetimes they have endured two waves of global recessions and a once-in-a-century (for now) global pandemic before the age of 35. Premature designations of this generation as "the lost generation" miss the mark by not adopting a strengths-based theoretical stance for understanding how young adults experience shocks and cultivate novel, adaptive approaches for making sense of these shock events as they discern who they want to be and where they want to go in life. (for further insights on research on generations, please see Mannheim,1952; Duffy, 2021; Rudolph, 2020). The findings derived from this research are noteworthy as these diverse students remained steadfast in their commitment to their postsecondary education plans, relying primarily upon proximal resources and supports. Those who referenced the specific supports outside of their residences primarily specified those that were within their postsecondary institutional settings. It is useful, then, to center the developmental properties of postsecondary education as foundational for positive identity outcomes. As such, it is important to interrogate the domain-specific effects of global exogenous shocks, not assuming homogenous effects observed at the aggregate level are true at the more localized levels immediately adjacent to individuals. For example, studying human development-centered readiness protocols at postsecondary institutions to promote adaptive coping responses during shocks will vary based on institutional funding and counseling resources. Further, the diversity of a school will necessitate activating culturally responsive interventions to improve effectiveness of supports. This is particularly important when considering the experiences of students of color in higher education and the need to promote their success in the wake of declining enrollment and completion rates (see Allen, McLewis, Jones, & Harris, 2018).

Postsecondary Institutions: Getting Their Bearings. While increased enrollment occurred during the peak period of the Great Recession, as noted in the introduction, these patterns belie other trends that frame this picture. Notably, people of color enrolled in college at a lesser rate than their White counterparts (see Figure 1.12). One of the more interesting effects of the Great Recession on higher education was that while institutions experienced increased enrollment, funding was down (Long, 2014). What is noteworthy is that many of the budget cuts put in place as a result of the Great Recession remained in place even after the economic shock was declared over, with 44 states spending less on post-secondary education between 2009 and 2017 (Mitchell, Michael, & Masterson, 2017). During COVID-19, the closure of postsecondary institutions produced another wave of shocks at a time when there was still scarring from the recovery from the Great Recession for many schools (Chronicle of Higher Education, April 10, 2020). As part of the broader U.S. federal stabilizing efforts, post-secondary institutions were recipients of nearly $50 billion in federal funds to ensure student learning continued. (U.S. Department of Education, 2021).

All of the participants in the qualitative component attended institutions that migrated to online learning environments which participants reported were not optimal (reported issues included distractions; loss of focus) expressing their preference for in-person instruction because attending courses via online portals did not meet all of their learning needs. Some participants noted their disconnection from their campus's traditions and resources as a source of risk for having the right information for managing their course taking plans. While for some college students the return home might be experienced as a backward movement in their search for autonomy, many semi-structured interview participants noted the ease of access to familial supports while at home. These varied experiences point to the importance of institutions to react in a timely matter to the myriad needs that emerge, influencing whether enrolled young adults are able to sustain engagement in a supportive context, or are forced to make other choices that derail their advancement to degree.

Beyond Postsecondary Education: Re-conceptualizing Work

Paradigm shifts resulting from recessions and public health emergencies have revealed a need to transform how work is defined and engaged when considering the life span implications of the linkage between education and work pursuits. After the Great Recession, the "gig" economy, with its emphasis on flexibility absent the security of a steady income with benefits, grew significantly. As the pandemic receded, more employers grappled with altering their work structures to move away from in-person to a remote or hybrid work-based economy, with implications for improved work-life balance for workers in some sectors, and increased employment precarity in other employment sectors that rely on providing support services (e.g. office building maintenance; restaurant workers). In short, the nature of work is undergoing its second transformation in less than 20 years. Research undertaken by the General Social Survey entailed conducting cognitive interviews to clarify how the terms "job" and "work" are understood (Smith, 2017; Dugoni, 2017) and provides a useful exemplar of how to ensure research is grounded in the meaning making of young adults as they assess their employment choices both during and after they complete their postsecondary education. Dugoni's report found that among the non-representative group of respondents, study subjects made distinctions between the "job they had," referring to a "more narrow, specific" construct linked to salary while "the work they do" was associated with tasks that connoted "the contribution made to others, how interesting the tasks were to them, or to the perceived value of work to society" (Dugoni, 2017, p. 13). When considering the digital nativity of the participants in the qualitative component, these are important distinctions that merit continued investigation as the tools and notions of work undergo historic changes in a post-COVID-19 world. This avoids reflexively carrying forward terms, concepts, and constructs out of habit and anchors the interpretation of these items to lived milieus at work at the time of the research.

Life Course Research and Developmental Contexts: Demographic Inflection Point

Erikson developed his epigenetic model of psychosocial identity development over the life course, in the post–World War II demographic boom of the mid-20th century when life expectancy in the U.S. was steadily increasing (National Center for Health Statistics, 2021). The National Center for Health Statistics' National Vital Statistics System, in its report of the provisional estimates for life expectancy in the U.S., finds an 18 month decrease in overall life expectancy in the U.S. population, declining to 77.3 years in 2020 from 78.8 years in 2019 (Arias, Tejada-Vera, Ahmad, & Kochanek, 2021). This one year drop, the largest since World War II, is a stark statistic that varies by race and sex, with the Black population in the U.S. experiencing the worst one-year drop in life expectancy since the Great Depression (71 years, 10 months) and the Hispanic population experiencing a drop in life expectancy by three years between 2019 and 2020. shifting downward from 81.8 years to 78.8, with COVID-19 a key driver for the decline for these groups (*Ibid.*).

These trends set a life course frame for assessing how context functions in support of healthy young adulthood experiences for diverse individuals. Lerner (1992), in acknowledging the dynamic, patterned relations that constitute lived contexts, posits the theory of "developmental contextualism" as a useful perspective that accommodates the interacting properties of the levels of analysis, i.e., systems, that are scrutinized in development research. He notes:

> When applied to the level of the individual, developmental contextualism stresses that neither variables belonging to levels of analysis lying within the person (e.g., biological or psychological ones) nor variables belonging to levels lying outside the person (i.e., involving either interpersonal, such as peer group relations or extra personal—institutional, or physical ecological—relations) are the primary basis—or cause—of the individual's functioning or development. Rather, the structure . . . of the system—the pattern of relations—at any given point in time . . . is the 'event' causing the person's functioning; and changes in the form of these relations are not the cause of developmental change. Simply, not only do 'A' and 'B' simultaneously

> influence one another, but any change in A or B is a function of the organization of variables within which they are embedded.
>
> (Lerner, 1992, p. 24).

When considering the effects of exogenous shocks on the attainment of postsecondary education, which constitutes a critical milestone for young adult identity formation, Lerner's concept of developmental contextualism provides an avenue for discerning the interactive properties of context. Should the lived environment be one in which the negative effects of inequality have disproportionately altered life chances for select groups, then the dysfunction of the system must be accounted for in a theoretically motivated investigation. While the applicability of Erikson's theory (Erikson, 1968) remains active and relevant in this research study, neither Erikson nor Lerner anticipated the unique considerations of shocks for the diverse young adult developmental phase accompanied by a decrease in the average length of the human lifespan. Additionally, the unique challenges and opportunities of online social, education, and work environments require revision of assumptions of the developmental implications of contexts where the nature of risk and supports are inverted and more difficult to discern.

Acknowledging the theories that emphasize the critical role of context in framing ego identity development over the life course (i.e., Bronfenbrenner, Spencer, Elder), this book builds on these perspectives and offers an expanded set of contextual considerations to define the dynamics of the issues encountered at the young adulthood developmental stage that frame identity developmental processes in shocks. As such, this book affirms 1) the presence of shocks as critical events in the chronosystem necessitate a dynamic, strengths-based theoretical stance that acknowledges the phenomenological person-context nature of human development; 2) shocks collide with pre-existing conditions of systemic economic and racial inequality, disrupting developmental contexts; 3) these dynamic disruptions necessitate the intentional provision of supports to institutional settings and enrolled young adults that are sufficiently adaptive and flexible in order to encourage sustained engagement with education and work goals, thereby cultivating adaptive coping and encouraging positive identity development among diverse young adults (this includes consideration of online-based supports); 4) methodological approaches implemented to investigate the particular effects of an exogenous shock benefit from a theoretically motivated, mixed-methods strategy to deepen insights on how diverse young adults make meaning of the shocks' impact on their identity-building endeavors; and 5) policy interventions that acknowledge and plan for shocks vis-à-vis diverse young adult positive identity needs can support young adults' navigation of shock-related disruptions through the application of a DESTID theoretical approach.

Looking Ahead with Promise

Nearly a decade after the Great Recession was declared over, the COVID-19 global pandemic and linked recession hurled the world into another state of shock with existential repercussions. Both the quantitative and qualitative components of this U.S.-based study revealed that enrolled young adult survey respondents to the PSID as well as the diverse enrolled participants in the qualitative study demonstrated a capacity to cope with the dynamic disruptive effects of the Great Recession and COVID-19 by leveraging supports to engage risks and challenges. The result was sustained engagement with and pursuit of their education and work plans, even as these underwent revision in response to how they made meaning of the dynamic changes precipitated by the pandemic shock. For the participants in the qualitative interviews, this finding is particularly noteworthy given that this diverse group of young adults has experienced two exogenous shocks in their adolescent and young adulthood periods of development.

From these data findings emerges a new theoretical approach to address the unique dynamic effects of shocks that impact diverse young adult identity development as it occurs in disrupted contexts. Informed by PVEST, DESTID provides a novel avenue of inquiry in which the achievement of a stable identity is aided by the understood presence of supports, and the pusuit of an identity-enhancing goal possesses a crucial protective quality that helps diverse young adults engage uncertainty and heightened risk.

In the years to come, it will be important to monitor the human development implications of shocks and support the meaning making processes that enhance positive identity development. As the experience of exogenous shocks during their postsecondary education is woven into the fabric of diverse young adults' personal history, embedded as events in their life course, it will be useful to learn how the experience shapes their understanding of themselves and identities as they advance across the life course.

In the face of these challenges, enrolled young adults studied here demonstrated an optimism for their futures by remaining committed to their educational goals. The Dynamic Ecological Systems Theory of Identity Development advanced here provides a shock-sensitive framework for the continued investigation of the dynamics of strengths-based identity development for diverse individuals while accounting for disrupted contexts impacted by shocks. Social science research broadly and developmental science specifically can serve all diverse young adults well by remaining attuned to investigating the provision of supports that promote strengths-based identity development and the provision of tools to cultivate adaptive strategies to effectively navigate disruptions and to advance human thriving after the shocks subside.

References

Allen, W. R., McLewis, C., Jones, C., & Harris, D. (2018). From Bakke to Fisher: African American Students in U.S. Higher Education over Forty Years. *RSF: The Russell Sage Foundation Journal of the Social Sciences*, *4*(6), 41–72. https://doi.org/10.7758/rsf.2018.4.6.03.

Arias, E., Tejada-Vera, B., Ahmad, F., & Kochanek, K. D. (2021). *Provisional life expectancy estimates for 2020. Vital Statistics Rapid Release; No 15*. Hyattsville, MD: National Center for Health Statistics.

Bronfenbrenner, U. (1993). The ecology of cognitive development: Research models and fugitive findings. In R. H. Wozniak & K. W. Fischer (Eds.), *Development in context: Acting and thinking in specific environments*. Hoboken, NJ: Lawrence Erlbaum Associates, Inc.

Centers for Disease Control and Prevention. (2023). COVID data tracker. Atlanta, GA: U.S. Department of Health and Human Services. Retrieved from https://covid.cdc.gov/covid-data-tracker

Cozzolino, E., Smith, C., & Crosnoe, R. (2018). Family related disparities in college enrollment across the great recession. *Sociological Perspectives, 61*(5), 689–710.

Duffy, B. (2021). *Generations: Does when you're born shape who you are?* London: Atlantic Books.

Dugoni, B. (2017). *Report on cognitive interviews conducted on proposed new items for the 2018 general social survey*. Chicago IL: NORC at the University of Chicago.

Elder, G. H. J., Bronfenbrenner, U., & Clausen, J. A. (1999). *Children of the great depression: Social change in life experience* (25th Anniversary ed.). Boulder, CO: Westview Press.

Erikson, E. H. (1968). *Identity: Youth and crisis*. New York: Norton and Company.

Francis, D. V., & Darity, W. A. Jr. (2021). Separate and unequal under one roof: How the legacy of racialized tracking perpetuates within-school segregation. *RSF: The Russell Sage Foundation Journal of the Social Sciences*, *7*(1), 187–202. https://doi.org.proxy.uchicago.edu/10.7758/rsf.2021.7.1.11.

Frankenberg, E., Ee, J., Ayscue, J. B., & Orfield, G. (2019). Harming our common future: America's segregated schools 65 years after Brown. www. civilrightsproject. ucla. edu, (research).

Franklin, J. H., Greenberg, J., & Pollack, L. H. (2009). Remembering Brown: A Tribute to John Hope Franklin. *Duke Forum for Law & Social Change*, *1*, 171–178.

Gaynor, T. S., Kang, S. C., & Williams, B. N. (2021). Segregated spaces and separated races: The relationship between state-sanctioned violence, place, and black identity. *RSF: The Russell Sage Foundation Journal of the Social Sciences,* *7*(1), 50–66. https://doi.org/10.7758/RSF.2021.7.1.04.

Lerner, R. M. (1992). Dialectics, developmental contextualism, and the further enhancement of theory about puberty and psychosocial development. *The Journal of Early Adolescence, 12*(4), 366–388.

Long, B. T. (2014). The financial crisis and college enrollment: How have students and their families responded? In J. R. Brown & C. M. Hoxby (Eds.), *How the financial crisis and great recession affected higher education*. Chicago: The University of Chicago Press.

Mannheim, K. (1952). *Essays on the sociology of knowledge*. Oxford: Oxford University Press.

Mitchell, M., Leachman, M., & Masterson, K. (2017). A lost decade in higher education funding state cuts have driven up tuition and reduced quality. *Center on Budget and Policy Priorities*. Retrieved from https://www.cbpp.org/sites/default/files/atoms/files/2017_higher_ed_8–22–17_final.pdf.

National Center for Health Statistics (NCHS). (2021). Age-adjusted Death Rates and Life Expectancy at Birth (Both Sexes, All Races): United States, 1900 to 2018 National Vital Statistics System, historical data, 1900–1998 (see https://www.cdc.gov/nchs/nvss/mortality_historical_data.htm); NCHS, National Vital Statistics System, mortality data (see http://www.cdc.gov/nchs/deaths.htm); and CDC WONDER (see http://wonder.cdc.gov)

Nau, M. D. (2016). *Whose financial crisis? How the great recession reshaped economic instability and inequality in the U.S.* Retrieved from http://search.ebscohost.com.proxy.uchicago.edu/login.aspx?direct=true&db=edsndl&AN=edsndl.oai.union.ndltd.org.OhioLink.oai.etd.ohiolink.edu.osu1458297758&site=eds-live&scope=site.

Panel Study of Income Dynamics, public use dataset. (2017). *Survey Research Center, Institute for Social Research*, University of Michigan, Ann Arbor, MI.

Plakhotnik, M. S., Volkova, N. V., Jiang, C., Yahiaoui, D., Pheiffer, G., McKay, K., Newman, S., & Reißig-Thust, S. (2021). The perceived impact of COVID-19 on student well-being and the mediating role of the university support: Evidence from France, Germany, Russia, and the UK. *Frontiers in Psychology*, *12*, 642689. https://doi.org/10.3389/fpsyg.2021.642689.

Reed Douglas, S. (2021). Harlan's Dissent: Citizenship, education, and the color-conscious constitution. *RSF: The Russell Sage Foundation Journal of the Social Sciences*, *7*(1), 148–165.

Rudolph, C. S., & Zacher, H. (2020). "The COVID-19 generation": A cautionary note. *Work, Aging and Retirement*, *6*(3), 139–145. https://doi.org/10.1093/worker/waaa009.

Smialek, J. (2020, June 17). A Fed President says systemic racism hurts the economy. *The New York Times*. Retrieved from https://www.nytimes.com/2020/06/17/business/economy/neel-kashkari-federal-reserve-racism.html

Smith, T. (2017). *GSS Methodological Report No. 127: Question wording experiments: Job satisfaction and the co-residence of adult children and their parents*. Chicago, IL: NORC at the University of Chicago.

Spencer, M. B., & Dowd, N. E. (Expected 2024). *Radical Brown: Keeping the promise to America's children*. Cambridge, MA: Harvard Education Press (Full Citation Pending).

U.S. Department of Education, Office of Postsecondary Education. (2021). *CARES Act: Higher education emergency relief fund*. Retrieved from https://www2.ed.gov/about/offices/list/ope/caresact.html.

U.S. General Accountability Office. (2022). Broadband National Strategy Needed to Guide Federal Efforts to Reduce Digital Divide (GAO-22-104611). Report to Congressional Requesters.

U.S. General Accountability Office. (2023, February 1). Closing the Digital Divide for Millions of Americans without Broadband. Watchblog: Following the American Dollar. https://www.gao.gov/blog/closing-digital-divide-millions-americans-without-broadband.

United States Government Accountability Office. (2022). Student loans: Education has increased federal cost estimates of direct loans by billions due to programmatic and other changes (GAO-22-105365). Report to Congressional Requesters.

Wong, J. (2020, April 10). How will the pandemic change higher education. The *Chronicle of Higher Education*, *66*(27).

Appendix

PSID Transition into Adulthood Supplement

Select Questionnaire Items Regarding Great Recession, Education, and Work, by Cohort

2005

Respondent age	Calculated based on preload data
Are you doing any work for money now?	1 Yes 5 No 8 DK 9 NA/Refused 0 Valid skip
Are you currently attending college?	1 Yes 5 No 8 DK 9 NA/Refused 0 Valid skip
Do you have plans to go back to school?	1 Yes 5 No 8 DK 9 NA/Refused 0 Valid skip

2007

Respondent age	Calculated based on preload data
Are you doing any work for money now?	1 Yes 5 No

	8 DK 9 NA/Refused 0 Valid skip
Are you currently attending college?	1 Yes 5 No 8 DK 9 NA/Refused 0 Valid skip
Do you have plans to go back to school?	1 Yes 5 No 8 DK 9 NA/Refused 0 Valid skip

2009

Respondent age	Calculated based on preload data
Are you doing any work for money now?	1 Yes 5 No 8 DK 9 NA/Refused 0 Valid skip
Are you currently attending college?	1 Yes 5 No 8 DK 9 NA/Refused 0 Valid skip
Do you have plans to go back to school?	1 Yes 5 No 8 DK 9 NA/Refused 0 Valid skip
Has the current recession led you to change your education plans?	1 Yes 5 No 6 Volunteered: Doesn't have education plans 8 DK 9 NA/Refused

How is that? (How has the current economic recession led you to change your educational plans?)

Dropped out of school	1 Dropped out of school 8 DK 9 NA/Refused 0 Valid Skip
Returned to or enrolled in school	1 Returned to or enrolled in school 8 DK 9 NA/Refused 0 Valid skip
Postponed returning to school	1 Postponed returning to school 8 DK 9 NA/Refused 0 Valid skip
Stayed in school	1 Stayed in school 8 DK 9 NA/Refused 0 Valid Skip
Changed Major	1 Changed Major 8 DK 9 NA/Refused 0 Valid Skip
Took out new loans or borrowed money	1 Took out new loans or borrowed money 8 DK 9 NA/Refused 0 Valid Skip
Other-Specify	1 Other-Specify 8 DK 9 NA/Refused 0 Valid Skip

2011

Respondent age	Calculated based on preload data
Are you doing any work for money now?	1 Yes 5 No 8 DK

	9 NA/Refused 0 Valid skip
Are you currently attending college?	1 Yes 5 No 8 DK 9 NA/Refused 0 Valid skip
Do you have plans to go back to school?	1 Yes 5 No 8 DK 9 NA/Refused 0 Valid skip
Has the current recession led you to change your education plans?	1 Yes 5 No 6 Volunteered: Doesn't have education plans 8 DK 9 NA/Refused

How is that? (How has the current economic recession led you to change your educational plans?)

Dropped out of school	1 Dropped out of school 8 DK 9 NA/Refused 0 Valid Skip
Returned to or enrolled in school	1 Returned to or enrolled in school 8 DK 9 NA/Refused 0 Valid skip
Postponed returning to school	1 Postponed returning to school 8 DK 9 NA/Refused 0 Valid skip
Stayed in school	1 Stayed in school 8 DK 9 NA/Refused 0 Valid Skip

Changed Major	1 Changed Major 8 DK 9 NA/Refused 0 Valid Skip
Took out new loans or borrowed money	1 Took out new loans or borrowed money 8 DK 9 NA/Refused 0 Valid Skip
Other-Specify	1 Other-Specify 8 DK 9 NA/Refused 0 Valid Skip

2013

Respondent age	Calculated based on preload data
Are you doing any work for money now?	1 Yes 5 No 8 DK 9 NA/Refused 0 Valid skip
Are you currently attending college?	1 Yes 5 No 8 DK 9 NA/Refused 0 Valid skip
Do you have plans to go back to school?	1 Yes 5 No 8 DK 9 NA/Refused 0 Valid skip
Has the current recession led you to change your schooling or education plans?	1 Yes 5 No 6 Volunteered: Doesn't have schooling or education plans 8 DK 9 NA/Refused

How is that? (How has the current economic recession led you to change your schooling educational plans?)

Dropped out of school	1 Dropped out of school 8 DK 9 NA/Refused 0 Valid Skip
Returned to or enrolled in school	1 Returned to or enrolled in school 8 DK 9 NA/Refused 0 Valid skip
Postponed returning to school	1 Postponed returning to school 8 DK 9 NA/Refused 0 Valid skip
Stayed in school	1 Stayed in school 8 DK 9 NA/Refused 0 Valid Skip
Changed Major	1 Changed Major 8 DK 9 NA/Refused 0 Valid Skip
Took out new loans or borrowed money	1 Took out new loans or borrowed money 8 DK 9 NA/Refused 0 Valid Skip
Other-Specify	1 Other-Specify 8 DK 9 NA/Refused 0 Valid Skip

Source: Panel Study of Income Dynamics, public use dataset, 2021

Study Flyer

Are you in school? Or Are you working?
Are you between the ages of 18 and 20?
Do you have something to say about your education or work experiences?

If you are **enrolled in school or working,** you are invited to be part of an important study to better understand the education and work experiences of 18- to 20-year-olds by participating in PESGR!

The purpose of PESGR is to learn more **about diverse young adults' experiences after graduating from high school**. The study will capture information about the education and work experiences of **18- to 20-year-olds** as well as how they are pursuing their life goals. The data provided by you as a study participant will help researchers better understand the experiences you are having during this period of your life, the transition to adulthood.

Participation in the study is completely **voluntary** and involves a **30-minute interview**. You will be asked general questions about yourself, your work and school experiences, and the plans you have for your next steps in education, work, or other plans you may have. You will receive a **$30 e-gift card in appreciation for your participation.**

If you are interested in participating, please email pesgr@uchicago.edu. **Thank you!**

Frequently Asked Questions: What is this study about?

The purpose of PESGR is to learn more about diverse young adults' experiences after graduating from high school. The study will capture information about the education and work experiences of 18- to 20-year-olds in the United States as well as how they are pursuing their life goals. The data provided by you as a study participant will help researchers better understand the experiences you are having during this period of your life, the transition to adulthood.

What does participation in PESGR involve?

After providing your consent, participation in PESGR involves completing a 30-minute interview over the phone. You will be asked to respond to questions about your education experiences and plans, your work experiences and plans, and your life goals. There will be no tests administered during the interview. With your permission, the interviews will be audio-recorded. You will receive a $30 e-gift card in appreciation for your participation.

When will the interviews happen?

The interviews will be scheduled at a time that is convenient for you and when you are available for a 30-minute conversation.

How long will the interview take?

The interview will take 30 minutes.

Will my answers be secure?

The recordings and interview transcriptions will reside on the University of Chicago's secure data server. Your name and contact information will be stored separately from your responses in this secure space. Neither your name nor any other identifying information (such as my voice or picture) will be used in presentations or in written products resulting from the study. At the close of the study, all recordings and data will be archived on a secure data server and password protected for 12 months. After that time the recordings will be destroyed, and the data securely archived.

Will I have to answer every question?

Participation is completely voluntary, and you can refuse to answer any question you do not wish to respond to.

What risk do I face by participating?

Your participation in this study does not involve any risk to you beyond that of everyday life. Please note that taking part in this research study may not benefit you personally, but we may learn new things that could help others better support persons your age.

What will happen to the information I give?

After the interview is over, the recording will be uploaded to a secure data server and transcribed. Data files will be identified only by a unique case number, not with your personal identifying information. All data processing, coding, and analysis will occur in a secure data environment and findings will be reported without personal identifying information (i.e., name, contact information). Neither your name nor your voice will be used in presentations or in written products resulting from the study. At the close of the study, all recordings and data will be archived on a secure data server and password protected for 12 months. After that time, the recordings will be destroyed, and the data securely archived.

Are my answers confidential?

Yes. The data is being captured for research purposes only. Neither your name, voice, or contact information will be sold or shared in reporting the study results. All data files will be housed on a secure data server at the University of Chicago, only identifiable by a unique identification number.

Will there be any follow up interviews?

No, the study only requires participation in only one (1) interview.

If you need further assistance, here are hotlines you can call:

USDA National Hunger Hotline—1-866-3-HUNGRY

National Hotline for Mental Health Support and/or Substance Use Disorders—1-800-662-HELP National Suicide Prevention Hotline—1-800-273-8255

Referral to housing counseling agency in your area—800-569-4287

PESGR Respondent Screener and Interview Protocol

PESGR Screener and Introductory Script:

Screener:

(Start Recording)

Can you please confirm that you have consented to my recording this interview? (*If Yes: proceed; If No: Thank respondent and end interview recording.*)

Can you confirm your birthdate? (*If R less than 18 years old or older than 20 years old:* You are not within the established selection criteria for participation. Thank you for participating in this screener.) *[End Call]*

Introductory Script:

If R is between 18 and 20 years old: Congratulations! You are eligible to participate in PESGR. Before proceeding, can you let me know if you require any accommodations to participate in an interview phone? (*Zoom if respondent preference.*) (*Proceed with call to schedule interview time when accommodations can be arranged or to conduct interview.*)

I have provided you a consent form which I can read to you out loud now or you may read now. (*After respondent has read the consent form or the consent form has been to them, ask*:).

READ CONSENT STATEMENT AND TWO AGREEMENT POINTS AT END OF CONSENT FORM

Participation is voluntary. Refusal to participate or withdrawing from the research will involve no penalty or loss of benefits to which you might otherwise be entitled. You have been provided a copy of this form. Do you agree to participate? (Yes/No) Do you agree to be recorded? (Yes/No)

Do I have your consent to proceed with the interview? *(if Yes: "Let's begin"; If No: Thank respondent for their time and end interview recording.)*

Thank you for agreeing to participate in PESGR. The information you provide will give researchers important insights on the education, work, and life experiences of 18- to 20-year-olds in the United States. Your participation is voluntary, and you may refuse to answer any question at any time. All responses you provide will be confidential and shared results for this study will not identify you personally. If you have any questions during this interview feel free to ask. The interview will take approximately 30 minutes.

PESGR Interview Protocol:

General Demographic/Background Questions:

The first set of questions are general demographic and background questions about you.

1. What is your racial/ethnic affiliation? (*respondents may offer more than one category*)
2. What is your sex/gender identity? (*open-ended question to allow for non-binary gender categories*)
3. Do you have any children? (*if yes: How many? How old are they?*)
4. Is there any other information about who you are, your background, or identity you wish to share?
5. What is the zip code where you currently reside? (*If applicable: What is zip code where your school is located? Work?*)

College Enrollment and Work Questions:

6. Are you currently attending college? If enrollment is confirmed: You're currently enrolled in college, correct? (*If yes: What year are you enrolled in currently? What is your major?; If no: Have you ever been enrolled in college? Do you plan to return to college?*)
7. Are you currently employed in a job for pay? (*If yes: What is your job? Is it full time, part time, or on-demand ["gig"]?*)

Effects of Economic Shock on Education Plans:

Now I'd like to shift to learn more about your education and work plans.

8. Has the current recession caused you to change your education plans? (*if yes: How is that?*)
9. Has current pandemic caused you to change your education plans? (*if yes: How is that?*)
10. What role does a college education play in where you want to go in your life?
11. What are the top three risks or challenges to achieving your education goals right now?
    (*Answering "None" is an acceptable response*)
12. What are the top three risks or challenges to achieving your work goals right now?
    (*Answering "None" is an acceptable response*)

Sources of Support and Resources:

For these final items, I would like to learn more about your resources and supports.

13. Resources refers to sources of income, healthcare, food, housing, or other things that help you meet your material daily needs. Do you consider your

life right now as being low resourced (not getting enough to meet daily needs), medium resourced (you're getting enough to meet daily needs), or high resourced (you have more than enough to meet your daily needs).

14. Supports can be persons, agencies, organizations, or other entities that help you meet your needs and navigate challenges. What kinds of supports help you cope with challenges or risks you are facing at school? At work?
15. How long does it take for you to access the most important supports to you?
16. Is there anything else you would like to share?

Thank you very much for your time!—END-
(*Obtain information to send R e-card*)

Index

Note: Page numbers in **bold** indicate a table and page numbers in *italics* indicate a figure on the corresponding page.

For Product Safety Concerns and Information please contact our EU representative GPSR@taylorandfrancis.com Taylor & Francis Verlag GmbH, Kaufingerstraße 24, 80331 München, Germany

Printed and bound by CPI Group (UK) Ltd, Croydon, CR0 4YY
14/09/2026
02216243-0019